Edward B. Cowell, F. Max Müller, Junj Takakusu

Buddhist Mahâyâna Texts

Volume 1

Edward B. Cowell, F. Max Müller, Junj Takakusu

Buddhist Mahâyâna Texts
Volume 1

ISBN/EAN: 9783337246877

Printed in Europe, USA, Canada, Australia, Japan

Cover: Foto ©Lupo / pixelio.de

More available books at **www.hansebooks.com**

THE
SACRED BOOKS OF THE EAST

TRANSLATED

BY VARIOUS ORIENTAL SCHOLARS

AND EDITED BY

F. MAX MÜLLER

VOL. XLIX

Oxford
AT THE CLARENDON PRESS
1894

[All rights reserved]

Oxford
PRINTED AT THE CLARENDON PRESS
BY HORACE HART, PRINTER TO THE UNIVERSITY

CONTENTS OF THE TWO PARTS.

BUDDHIST MAHÂYÂNA TEXTS.

PART I.

	PAGE
INTRODUCTION	ix
THE BUDDHA-KARITA OF ASVAGHOSHA: BOOKS I–XVII	1
INDEX OF PROPER NAMES	203
NOTES AND CORRECTIONS . .	207

Translated by E. B. COWELL.

PART II.

INTRODUCTION	v
1. THE LARGER SUKHÂVATÎ-VYÛHA .	1
INDEX OF WORDS . .	77
INDEX OF SUBJECTS . .	85
2. THE SMALLER SUKHÂVATÎ-VYÛHA .	87
INDEX OF NAMES AND SUBJECTS	105
INDEX OF SANSKRIT WORDS .	107
3. THE VAGRAKKHEDIKÂ	109
4. THE LARGER PRAGÑÂ-PÂRAMITÂ-HRIDAYA-SÛTRA	145
5. THE SMALLER PRAGÑÂ-PÂRAMITÂ-HRIDAYA-SÛTRA .	151
INDEX OF NAMES AND SUBJECTS	155
INDEX OF SANSKRIT WORDS . .	157

Translated by F. MAX MÜLLER.

6. THE AMITÂYUR-DHYÂNA-SÛTRA .	159
INDEX OF NAMES AND SUBJECTS .	203

Translated by J. TAKAKUSU.

Transliteration of Oriental Alphabets adopted for the Translations of the Sacred Books of the East .	205

THE BUDDHA-*K*ARITA

OF

ASVAGHOSHA

TRANSLATED FROM THE SANSKRIT

BY

E. B. COWELL

Oxford

AT THE CLARENDON PRESS

1894

[*All rights reserved*]

INTRODUCTION.

The Sanskrit text of the Buddha-karita was published at the beginning of last year in the 'Anecdota Oxoniensia,' and the following English translation is now included in the series of 'Sacred Books of the East.' It is an early Sanskrit poem written in India on the legendary history of Buddha, and therefore contains much that is of interest for the history of Buddhism, beside its special importance as illustrating the early history of classical Sanskrit literature.

It is ascribed to Asvaghosha; and, although there were several writers who bore that name, it seems most probable that our author was the contemporary and spiritual adviser of Kanishka in the first century of our era. Hiouen Thsang, who left India in A.D. 645, mentions him with Deva, Nâgârguna, and Kumâralabdha, 'as the four suns which illumine the world[1];' but our fullest account is given by I-tsing, who visited India in 673. He states that Asvaghosha was an ancient author who composed the Alamkâra-sâstra and the Buddha-karita-kâvya,—the latter work being of course the present poem. Beside these two works he also composed the hymns in honour of Buddha and the three holy beings Amitâbha, Avalokitesvara, and Mahâsthâma, which were chanted at the evening service of the monasteries. 'In the five countries of India and in the countries of the Southern ocean they recite these poems, because they express a store of ideas and meaning in a few words[2].' A solitary stanza (VIII, 13) is

---

[1] Julien's Translation, vol. ii, p. 214.
[2] See M. Fujishama, Journal Asiatique, 1888, p. 425.

quoted from the Buddha-*k*arita in Râyamuku*t*a's commentary on the Amarakosha I, 1. 1, 2, and also by Ug*g*valadatta in his commentary on the U*n*âdi-sûtras I, 156; and five stanzas are quoted as from A*s*vaghosha in Vallabhadeva's Subhâshitâvali, which bear a great resemblance to his style, though they are not found in the extant portion of this poem [1].

The Buddha-*k*arita was translated into Chinese [2] by Dharmaraksha in the fifth century, and a translation of this was published by the Rev. S. Beal in the present series; it was also translated into Tibetan in the seventh or eighth century. The Tibetan as well as the Chinese version consists of twenty-eight chapters, and carries down the life of Buddha to his entrance into Nirvâ*n*a and the subsequent division of the sacred relics. The Tibetan version appears to be much closer to the original Sanskrit than the Chinese; in fact from its verbal accuracy we can often reproduce the exact words of the original, since certain Sanskrit words are always represented by the same Tibetan equivalents, as for instance the prepositions prefixed to verbal roots. I may here express an earnest hope that we may still ere long have an edition and translation of the Tibetan version, if some scholar can be found to complete Dr. Wenzel's unfinished labour. He had devoted much time and thought to the work; I consulted him in several of my difficulties, and it is from him that I derived all my information about the Tibetan renderings. This Tibetan version promises to be of great help in restoring the many corrupt readings which still remain in our faulty Nepalese MSS.

Only thirteen books of the Sanskrit poem claim to be A*s*vaghosha's composition; the last four books are an attempt by a modern Nepalese author to supply the loss of the original. He tells us this honestly in the colophon,

---

[1] Professor Peterson has remarked that two stanzas out of the five occur in Bhart*r*ihari's Nîti-*s*ataka.

[2] We have for the present classed the Buddha-*k*arita with the Mahâyâna Sûtras in default of more exact information.

—'having searched for them everywhere and not found them, four cantos have been made by me, Amr*i*tânanda,— the fourteenth, fifteenth, sixteenth, and seventeenth.' He adds the date 950 of the Nepalese era, corresponding to 1830 A.D.; and we have no difficulty in identifying the author. Râ*g*endralâl Mitra in his 'Nepalese Buddhist Literature' mentions Amr*i*tânanda as the author of two Sanskrit treatises and one in Newârî; he was probably the father of the old pa*nd*it of the Residency at Kâ*t*mâ*nd*u, Gu*n*ânanda, whose son Indrânanda holds the office at present. Dr. D. Wright informs me that the family seem to have been the recognised historians of the country, and keepers of the MS. treasures of sundry temples. The four books are included in this translation as an interesting literary curiosity. The first portion of the fourteenth book agrees partly with the Tibetan and Chinese, and Amr*i*tânanda may have had access to some imperfect copy of this portion of the original; but after that his account is quite independent, and has no relation to the two versions.

In my preface to the edition of the Sanskrit text I have tried to show that A*s*vaghosha's poem appears to have exercised an important influence on the succeeding poets of the classical period in India. When we compare the description in the seventh book of the Raghuva*ms*a of the ladies of the city crowding to see prince A*g*a as he passes by from the Svaya*m*vara where the princess Bho*g*yâ has chosen him as her husband, with the episode in the third book of the Buddha-*k*arita (*s*lokas 13-24); or the description of Kâma's assault on *S*iva in the Kumârasa*m*bhava with that of Mâra's temptation of Buddha in the thirteenth book, we can hardly fail to trace some connection. There is a similar resemblance between the description in the fifth book of the Râmâya*n*a, where the monkey Hanumat enters Râva*n*a's palace by night, and sees his wives asleep in the seraglio and their various unconscious attitudes, and the description in the fifth book of the present poem where Buddha on the night of his leaving his home for ever sees the same unconscious sight in his own palace. Nor may we forget that in the Râmâyana the description is merely introduced as an ornamental episode; in the Buddhist poem it is an essential element in the story, as it supplies the final impulse which stirs the Bodhisattva to make his escape from the world. These different descriptions became afterwards commonplaces in Sanskrit poetry, like the catalogue of the ships in Greek or Roman epics; but they may very well have originated in connection with definite incidents in the Buddhist sacred legend.

The Sanskrit MSS. of Nepal are always negligently transcribed and abound with corrupt passages, which it is often very difficult to detect and restore. My printed text leaves many obscure lines which will have to be cleared up hereafter by more skilful emendations. I have given in the notes to the translation some further emendations of my own, and I have also added several happy conjectures which continental scholars have kindly suggested to me by letter; and I gladly take this opportunity of adding in a foot-note some which I received too late to insert in their proper places [1].

I have endeavoured to make my translation intelligible to the English reader, but many of the verses in the original are very obscure. Asvaghosha employs all the resources of Hindu rhetoric (as we might well expect if I-tsing is right in ascribing to him an 'alamkâra-sâstra'), and it is often difficult to follow his subtil turns of thought and remote allusions; but many passages no doubt owe their present obscurity to undetected mistakes in the text of our MSS. In the absence of any commentary (except so far as the diffuse Chinese translation and occasional reference to the Tibetan have supplied the want) I have been necessarily left to my own resources, and I cannot fail to have sometimes missed my author's meaning,

Prâmsulabhye phale mohâd udbâhur iva vâmanah;

---

[1] Dr. von Boehtlingk suggests 'saugā vikakâra' in VIII, 3, and 'vilambakesyo' in VIII, 21,—two certain emendations. Professor Kielhorn would read 'nabhasy eva' in XIII, 47 for 'nayaty eva,' and 'tatraiva nâsînam rishim' in XIII, 50. Professor Bühler would read 'priyatanayas tanayasya' in I, 87, and 'na tatyâga ka' in IV, 80.

but I have tried to do my best, and no one will welcome more cordially any light which others may throw on the passages which I have misunderstood.

The edition of the original text was dedicated to my old friend Professor F. Max Müller, and it is a sincere gratification to me that this translation will appear in the same volume with similar translations from his pen.

E. B. C.

CAMBRIDGE:
Feb. 1, 1894.

THE BUDDHA-*K*ARITA

OF

A*S*VAGHOSHA.

THE BUDDHA-*K*ARITA

OF

A*S*VAGHOSHA.

BOOK I.

1. That Arhat is here saluted, who has no counterpart,—who, as bestowing the supreme happiness, surpasses (Brahman) the Creator,—who, as driving away darkness, vanquishes the sun,—and, as dispelling all burning heat, surpasses the beautiful moon.

2. There was a city, the dwelling-place[1] of the great saint Kapila, having its sides surrounded by the beauty of a lofty broad table-land as by a line of clouds, and itself, with its high-soaring palaces[2], immersed in the sky.

3. By its pure and lofty system of government it, as it were, stole the splendour of the clouds of Mount Kailâsa, and while it bore the clouds which came to it through a mistake, it fulfilled the imagination which had led them thither[3].

4. In that city, shining with the splendour of gems, darkness like poverty could find no place;

---

[1] Vastu seems used here for vâstu.   [2] Dhish*n*ya.
[3] They had thought that it was Kailâsa.

prosperity shone resplendently, as with a smile, from the joy of dwelling with such surpassingly excellent citizens.

5. With its festive arbours, its arched gateways and pinnacles [1], it was radiant with jewels in every dwelling; and unable to find any other rival in the world, it could only feel emulation with its own houses.

6. There the sun, even although he had retired, was unable to scorn the moon-like faces of its women which put the lotuses to shame, and as if from the access of passion, hurried towards the western ocean to enter the (cooling) water.

7. 'Yonder Indra has been utterly annihilated by the people when they saw the glories [2] acquired by the Sâkyas,'—uttering this scoff, the city strove by its banners with gay-fluttering streamers to wipe away every mark of his existence.

8. After mocking the water-lilies even at night by the moonbeams which rest on its silver pavilions,—by day it assumed the brightness of the lotuses through the sunbeams falling on its golden palaces.

9. A king, by name Suddhodana, of the kindred of the sun, anointed to stand at the head of earth's monarchs,—ruling over the city, adorned it, as a bee-inmate a full-blown lotus [3].

10. The very best of kings with his train ever

---

[1] Or towers? (simhakarnaih).
[2] For the genitive yasasâm, see Pân. II, 3. 52 (adhîgartha).
[3] Vâ is used for iva in Sisup. Badha, III, 63, IV, 35; Meghad. 82. (Cf. infra, IV, 44.) Purâdhirâgam seems used adverbially. Cf. the line in Vikramorv. kusumâny âsrate shatpadâh. Could it mean 'as a thought the lotus of the heart?'

near him [1],—intent on liberality yet devoid of pride [2]; a sovereign, yet with an ever equal eye thrown on all [3],—of gentle nature and yet with wide-reaching majesty [4].

11. Falling smitten by his arm in the arena of battle, the lordly elephants of his enemies bowed prostrate with their heads pouring forth quantities of pearls as if they were offering handfuls of flowers in homage.

12. Having dispersed his enemies by his preeminent majesty as the sun disperses the gloom of an eclipse, he illuminated his people on every side, showing them the paths which they were to follow.

13. Duty, wealth, and pleasure under his guidance assumed mutually each other's object, but not the outward dress; yet as if they still vied together they shone all the brighter in the glorious career of their triumphant success.

14. He, the monarch of the *S*âkyas, of native pre-eminence, but whose actual pre-eminence was brought about by his numberless councillors of exalted wisdom, shone forth all the more gloriously, like the moon amidst the stars shining with a light like its own [5].

15. To him there was a queen, named Mâyâ, as if free from all deceit (mâyâ)—an effulgence proceeding

---

[1] Also 'though the highest of mountains, yet bearing his wings (uncut).'

[2] Or if applied to an elephant, 'not in rut.'

[3] Or with a double meaning in îsa, 'though like *S*iva, yet with even eyes,' i.e. not three.

[4] Or 'like the moon, yet widely burning (like the sun).'

[5] Or perhaps ' shining with undiminished splendour.' If we read akr*i*tânyathâbha*h* it would run, 'shining with its light undimmed by the stars.'

from his effulgence, like the splendour of the sun when it is free from all the influence of darkness,—a chief queen in the united assembly of all queens.

16. Like a mother to her subjects, intent on their welfare,—devoted to all worthy of reverence like devotion itself,—shining on her lord's family like the goddess of prosperity,—she was the most eminent of goddesses to the whole world.

17. Verily the life of women is always darkness, yet when it encountered her, it shone brilliantly; thus the night does not retain its gloom, when it meets with the radiant crescent of the moon.

18. 'This people, being hard to be roused to wonder in their souls, cannot be influenced by me if I come to them as beyond their senses,'—so saying, Duty abandoned her own subtile nature and made her form visible.

19. Then falling from the host of beings in the Tushita heaven [1], and illumining the three worlds, the most excellent of Bodhisattvas suddenly entered at a thought into her womb, like the Nâga-king entering the cave of Nandâ.

20. Assuming the form of a huge elephant white like Himâlaya, armed with six tusks [2], with his face perfumed with flowing ichor, he entered the womb of the queen of king Suddhodana, to destroy the evils of the world.

21. The guardians of the world hastened from heaven to mount watch over the world's one true ruler; thus the moonbeams, though they shine

---

[1] For tushitât kâyât, cf. tushite devanikâya upapannâ, Divyâvad. p. 83; and tushitakâyika, Lalitav. p. 142.

[2] Cf. the Pâli khaddanto, and the Lalitav. shaddanta.

everywhere, are especially bright on Mount Kailâsa.

22. Mâyâ also, holding him in her womb, like a line of clouds holding a lightning-flash, relieved the people around her from the sufferings of poverty by raining showers of gifts.

23. Then one day by the king's permission the queen, having a great longing in her mind, went with the inmates of the gynaeceum into the garden Lumbinî.

24. As the queen supported herself by a bough which hung laden with a weight of flowers, the Bodhisattva suddenly came forth, cleaving open her womb.

25. [1] At that time the constellation Pushya was auspicious, and from the side of the queen, who was purified by her vow, her son was born for the welfare of the world, without pain and without illness.

26. Like the sun bursting from a cloud in the morning,—so he too, when he was born from his mother's womb, made the world bright like gold, bursting forth with his rays which dispelled the darkness.

27. As soon as he was born the thousand-eyed (Indra) well-pleased took him gently, bright like a golden pillar; and two pure streams of water fell down from heaven upon his head with piles of Mandâra flowers.

28. Carried about by the chief suras, and delighting them with the rays that streamed from his body, he

---

[1] From this point the Tibetan and Chinese versions agree more or less closely with the Sanskrit text.

surpassed in beauty the new moon as it rests on a mass of evening clouds.

29. As was Aurva's birth from the thigh [1], and Prithu's from the hand [2], and Mândhâtri's, who was like Indra himself, from the forehead [3], and Kakshîvat's from the upper end of the arm [4],—thus too was his birth (miraculous).

30. Having thus in due time issued from the womb, he shone as if he had come down from heaven, he who had not been born in the natural way,—he who was born full of wisdom, not foolish,—as if his mind had been purified by countless aeons of contemplation.

31. With glory, fortitude, and beauty he shone like the young sun descended upon the earth; when he was gazed at, though of such surpassing brightness, he attracted all eyes like the moon.

32. With the radiant splendour of his limbs he extinguished like the sun the splendour of the lamps; with his beautiful hue as of precious gold he illuminated all the quarters of space.

33. Unflurried, with the lotus-sign in high relief [5], far-striding, set down with a stamp,—seven such firm footsteps did he then take,—he who was like the constellation of the seven rishis.

34. 'I am born for supreme knowledge, for the welfare of the world,—thus this is my last birth,'—

---

[1] Mahâbh. I, 2610.   [2] Vishnu Pur. I, 13.

[3] According to the Mahâbh. III, l. 10450, he was born from his father's left side, but cf. Vishnu Pur. IV, 2.

[4] The MSS. vary between bhugâmsa and bhugamsa; we might conjecture bhugâgradesât, but bhugâmsadesât is the only reading in V, 56. Beal I, 10 has 'the armpit.'

[5] Abgasamudgatâni. Cf. Beal I, 16, note.

thus did he of lion gait, gazing at the four quarters, utter a voice full of auspicious meaning.

35. Two streams of water bursting from heaven, bright as the moon's rays, having the power of heat and cold, fell down upon that peerless one's benign head to give refreshment to his body.

36. His body lay on a bed with a royal canopy and a frame shining with gold, and supported by feet of lapis lazuli, and in his honour the yaksha-lords stood round guarding him with golden lotuses in their hands.

37. The gods in homage to the son of Mâyâ, with their heads bowed at his majesty, held up a white umbrella in the sky and muttered the highest blessings on his supreme wisdom.

38. The great dragons[1] in their great thirst for the Law[2],—they who had had the privilege of waiting on the past Buddhas,—gazing with eyes of intent devotion, fanned[3] him and strewed Mandâra flowers over him.

39. Gladdened through the influence of the birth of the Tathâgata, the gods of pure natures and inhabiting pure abodes[4] were filled with joy, though all passion was extinguished, for the sake of the world[5] drowned in sorrow.

40. When he was born, the earth, though fastened down by (Himâlaya) the monarch of mountains, shook like a ship tossed by the wind; and from a cloudless sky there fell a shower full of lotuses and water-lilies, and perfumed with sandal-wood.

---

[1] Mahoragâ*h*.
[2] Cf. infra, *s*loka 54.
[3] Avya*g*an.
[4] *S*uddhâdhivâsâ*h*.
[5] Reading hitâya.

41. Pleasant breezes blew soft to the touch, dropping down heavenly garments; the very sun, though still the same, shone with augmented light, and fire gleamed, unstirred, with a gentle lustre.

42. In the north-eastern part of the dwelling a well of pure water appeared of its own accord, wherein the inhabitants of the gynaeceum, filled with wonder, performed their rites as in a sacred bathing-place.

43. Through the troops of heavenly visitants, who came seeking religious merit, the pool itself received strength to behold Buddha, and by means of its trees bearing flowers and perfumes it eagerly offered him worship.

44. The flowering trees at once produced their blossoms, while their fragrance was borne aloft in all directions by the wind, accompanied by the songs of bewildered female bees, while the air was inhaled and absorbed by the many snakes (gathering near)[1].

45. Sometimes there resounded[2] on both sides songs mingled with musical instruments and tabours, and lutes also, drums, tambourines, and the rest,— from women adorned with dancing bracelets.

46. '[3] That royal law which neither Bh*r*igu nor A*n*giras ever made, those two great seers the founders of families, their two sons *S*ukra and V*ri*haspati left revealed at the end.

---

[1] Serpents are called vâyubhaksha. See Ind. Sprüche, III, 4738, and Raghuva*m*sa XIII, 12. Cf. also infra, VII, 15.

[2] Virâgitam, 'it was manifested by.' Can tat mean 'then' or 'there?'

[3] We learn from *s*loka 52 that this is a speech uttered by the Brahmans of the court.

47. 'Yea, the son of Sarasvatî[1] proclaimed that lost Veda which they had never seen in former ages,—Vyâsa rehearsed that in many forms, which Va*sish*t*h*a helpless could not compile;

48. 'The voice of Vâlmîki uttered its poetry which the great seer *K*yavana could not compose; and that medicine which Atri never invented the wise son of Atri[2] proclaimed after him;

49. 'That Brahmanhood which Ku*s*ika never attained,—his son, O king, found out the means to gain it; (so) Sagara made a bound for the ocean, which even the Ikshvâkus had not fixed before him.

50. '*G*anaka attained a power of instructing the twice-born in the rules of Yoga which none other had ever reached[3]; and the famed feats of the grandson of *S*ûra[4] (K*rish*n*a*) *S*ûra and his peers were powerless to accomplish.

51. 'Therefore it is not age nor years which are the criterion; different persons win pre-eminence in the world at different places; those mighty exploits worthy of kings and sages, when left undone by the ancestors, have been done by the sons.'

52. The king, being thus consoled and congratulated by those well-trusted Brahmans, dismissed from his mind all unwelcome suspicion and rose to a still higher degree of joy;

53. And well-pleased he gave to those most excellent of the twice-born rich treasures with all

---

[1] The Vish*n*u Pur. (III, 3) says that Sârasvata arranged the Vedas in the ninth age, as Va*sish*t*h*a in the eighth.

[2] Âtreya is the proclaimer of the *K*araka-sa*m*hitâ.

[3] Cf. *Kh*ândogya Upan. V, 3, 7.

[4] Read *S*aure*h* for *S*aurai*h*.

due honour,—'May he become the ruler of the earth according to your words, and may he retire to the woods when he attains old age.'

54. Then having learned by signs and through the power of his penances this birth of him who was to destroy all birth, the great seer Asita in his thirst for the excellent Law[1] came to the palace of the *S*âkya king.

55. Him shining with the glory of sacred knowledge and ascetic observances, the king's own priest,—himself a special student among the students of sacred knowledge,—introduced into the royal palace with all due reverence and respect.

56. He entered into the precincts of the king's gynaeceum, which was all astir with the joy arisen from the birth of the young prince,—grave from his consciousness of power, his pre-eminence in asceticism, and the weight of old age.

57. Then the king, having duly honoured the sage, who was seated in his seat, with water for the feet and an arghya offering, invited him (to speak) with all ceremonies of respect, as did Antideva[2] in olden time to Va*s*ish*th*a:

58. 'I am indeed fortunate, this my family is the object of high favour, that thou shouldst have come to visit me; be pleased to command what I should do, O benign one; I am thy disciple, be pleased to show thy confidence in me.'

59. The sage, being thus invited by the king, filled with intense feeling as was due, uttered his

---

[1] Cf. *s*loka 38 *a*.
[2] See IX, 20, 60. C reads Atideva, i.e. Indra? [The Tibetan reads Antadeva, 'in the end dwelling god' or 'end having god.' H. W.]

deep and solemn words, having his large eyes opened wide with wonder:

60. 'This is indeed worthy of thee, great-souled as thou art, fond of guests, liberal and a lover of duty,—that thy mind should be thus kind towards me, in full accordance with thy nature, family, wisdom, and age.

61. 'This is the true way in which those seer-kings of old, rejecting through duty all trivial riches[1], have ever flung them away as was right,—being poor in outward substance but rich in ascetic endurance.

62. 'But hear now the motive for my coming and rejoice thereat; a heavenly voice has been heard by me in the heavenly path, that thy son has been born for the sake of supreme knowledge.

63. 'Having heard that voice and applied my mind thereto, and having known its truth by signs, I am now come hither, with a longing to see the banner of the *S*âkya race, as if it were Indra's banner being set up[2].'

64. Having heard this address of his, the king, with his steps bewildered with joy, took the prince, who lay on his nurse's side, and showed him to the holy ascetic.

65. Thus the great seer beheld the king's son with wonder,—his foot marked with a wheel, his fingers and toes webbed, with a circle of hair between his eyebrows, and signs of vigour like an elephant.

66. Having beheld him seated on his nurse's side,

---

[1] Or 'all riches which were trifling in comparison with duty.'

[2] In allusion to a festival in parts of India; cf. Schol. Raghuva*m*sa IV, 3. (Cf. Mrs. Guthrie's Year in an Indian Fort, vol. ii.)

like the son of Agni (Skanda) seated on Devî's side, he stood with the tears hanging on the ends of his eyelashes[1], and sighing he looked up towards heaven.

67. But seeing Asita with his eyes thus filled with tears, the king was agitated through his love for his son, and with his hands clasped and his body bowed he thus asked him in a broken voice choked with weeping,

68. 'One whose beauty has little to distinguish it from that of a divine sage[2], and whose brilliant birth has been so wonderful, and for whom thou hast prophesied a transcendent future,—wherefore, on seeing him, do tears come to thee, O reverend one?

69. 'Is the prince, O holy man, destined to a long life? Surely he cannot be born for my sorrow[3]. I have with difficulty obtained a handful of water, surely it is not death which comes to drink it.

70. 'Tell me, is the hoard of my fame free from destruction? Is this chief prize of my family secure? Shall I ever depart happily to another life,—I who keep one eye ever awake, even when my son is asleep[4]?

71. 'Surely this young shoot of my family is not born barren, destined only to wither! Speak quickly, my lord, I cannot wait; thou well knowest the love of near kindred for a son.'

72. Knowing the king to be thus agitated through his fear of some impending evil, the sage thus ad-

---

[1] I adopt Prof. Kielhorn's suggestion, pakshmântavilambitâsruh. (Aṅkita might mean 'curved on his eyelashes.')

[2] Or, reading mune, 'one whose age is so small, O sage.'

[3] Kakkinna sokâya mama prasûtah.   [4] Obscure.

dressed him: 'Let not thy mind, O monarch, be disturbed,—all that I have said is certainly true[1].

73. 'I have no feeling of fear as to his being subject to change, but I am distressed for mine own disappointment. It is my time to depart, and this child is now born,—he who knows that mystery hard to attain, the means of destroying birth.

74. 'Having forsaken his kingdom, indifferent to all worldly objects, and having attained the highest truth by strenuous efforts, he will shine forth as a sun of knowledge to destroy the darkness of illusion in the world.

75. 'He will deliver by the boat of knowledge the distressed world, borne helplessly along, from the ocean of misery which throws up sickness as its foam, tossing with the waves of old age, and rushing with the dreadful onflow of death.

76. 'The thirsty world of living beings will drink the flowing stream of his Law, bursting forth with the water of wisdom, enclosed by the banks of strong moral rules, delightfully cool with contemplation, and filled with religious vows as with ruddy geese.

77. 'He will proclaim the way of deliverance to those afflicted with sorrow, entangled in objects of sense, and lost in the forest-paths of worldly existence, as to travellers who have lost their way.

78. 'By the rain of the Law he will give gladness to the multitude who are consumed in this world with that fire of desire whose fuel is worldly objects, as a great cloud does with its showers at the end of the hot season.

---

[1] I take asmi as meaning aham (aham ityarthâvyayam), or should we read asti?

79. 'He will break open for the escape of living beings that door whose bolt is desire and whose two leaves are ignorance and delusion,—with that excellent blow of the good Law which is so hard to find.

80. 'He, the king of the Law, when he has attained to supreme knowledge, will achieve the deliverance from its bonds of the world now overcome by misery, destitute of every refuge, and enveloped in its own chains of delusion.

81. 'Therefore make no sorrow for him,—that belongs rather, kind sire, to the pitiable world of human beings, who through illusion or the pleasures of desire or intoxication refuse to hear his perfect Law.

82. 'Therefore since I have fallen short of that excellence, though I have accomplished all the stages of contemplation, my life is only a failure; since I have not heard his Law, I count even dwelling in the highest heaven a misfortune.'

83. Having heard these words, the king with his queen and his friends abandoned sorrow and rejoiced; thinking, 'such is this son of mine,' he considered that his excellence was his own.

84. But he let his heart be influenced by the thought, 'he will travel by the noble path,'—he was not in truth averse to religion, yet still he saw alarm at the prospect of losing his child.

85. Then the sage Asita, having made known the real fate which awaited the prince to the king who was thus disturbed about his son, departed by the way of the wind as he had come, his figure watched reverentially in his flight.

86. Having taken his resolution and having seen

the son of his younger sister¹, the saint, filled with compassion, enjoined him earnestly in all kinds of ways, as if he were his son, to listen to the sage's words and ponder over them.

87. The monarch also, being well-pleased at the birth of a son, having thrown off all those bonds called worldly objects, caused his son to go through the usual birth-ceremonies in a manner worthy of the family.

88. When ten days were fulfilled after his son's birth, with his thoughts kept under restraint, and filled with excessive joy, he offered for his son most elaborate sacrifices to the gods with muttered prayers, oblations, and all kinds of auspicious ceremonies.

89. And he himself gave to the brahmans for his son's welfare cows full of milk, with no traces of infirmity, golden-horned and with strong healthy calves, to the full number of a hundred thousand.

90. Then he, with his soul under strict restraint, having performed all kinds of ceremonies which rejoiced his heart, on a fortunate day, in an auspicious moment, gladly determined to enter his city.

91. Then the queen with her babe having worshipped the gods for good fortune, occupied a costly palanquin made of elephants' tusks, filled with all kinds of white flowers, and blazing with gems.

92. Having made his wife with her child² enter first into the city, accompanied by the aged attendants, the king himself also advanced, saluted by the

---

[1] This was Naradatta, see Lalitavistara, ch. vii. pp. 103, 110 (Foucaux).

[2] Apatyanâthâm might also mean 'having her child as her protector.'

hosts of the citizens, as Indra entering heaven, saluted by the immortals.

93. The *S*âkya king, having entered his palace, like Bhava [1] well-pleased at the birth of Kârttikeya [2], with his face full of joy, gave orders for lavish expenditure, showing all kinds of honour and liberality [3].

94. Thus at the good fortune of the birth of the king's son, that city surnamed after Kapila, with all the surrounding inhabitants, was full of gladness like the city of the lord of wealth [4], crowded with heavenly nymphs, at the birth of his son Nalakûvara.

---

[1] Sc. *S*iva. [2] Sha*n*mukha.
[3] Bahuvidhapush*t*iya*s*askaram seems used as an adverb to vyadhatta, 'he made expenditure.'
[4] Kuvera.

BOOK II.

1. From the time of the birth of that son of his, who, the true master of himself, was to end all birth and old age, the king increased day by day in wealth, elephants, horses, and friends as a river increases with its influx of waters.

2. Of different kinds of wealth and jewels, and of gold, wrought or unwrought, he found[1] treasures of manifold variety[2], surpassing even the capacity of his desires.

3. Elephants from Himavat, raging with rut, whom not even princes of elephants like Padma[3] could teach to go round in circles, came without any effort and waited on him.

4. His city was all astir with the crowds of horses, some adorned with various marks and decked with new golden trappings, others unadorned and with long flowing manes,—suitable alike in strength, gentleness, and costly ornaments[4].

5. And many fertile cows, with tall calves, gathered in his kingdom, well nourished and happy,

---

[1] I suppose avâpi to be used as a middle aorist like abodhi (cf. *Śiśup.* I, 3). Should we read avâpa?

[2] I take naikâtman as 'of manifold nature.'

[3] Mahâpadma is the name of the elephant which supports the world in the south.

[4] I read âptaiħ.

gentle and without fierceness, and producing excellent milk.

6. His enemies became indifferent; indifference grew into friendship; his friends became specially united; were there two sides,—one passed into oblivion.

7. Heaven rained in his kingdom in due time and place, with the sound of gentle winds and clouds, and adorned with wreaths of lightning, and without any drawback of showers of stones or thunderbolts.

8. A fruitful crop sprang up according to season, even without the labour of ploughing [1]; and the old plants grew more vigorous in juice and substance.

9. Even at that crisis which threatens danger to the body like the collision of battle, pregnant women brought forth in good health, in safety, and without sickness.

10. And whereas men do not willingly ask from others, even where a surety's property is available [2],—at that time even one possessed of slender means turned not his face away when solicited.

11. There was no ruin nor murder [3],—nay, there was not even one ungenerous to his kinsmen, no breaker of obligations, none untruthful nor injurious,—as in the days of Yayâti the son of Nahusha.

12. Those who sought religious merit performed sacred works and made gardens, temples, and

---

[1] Tadâ·krítenâpi kríshisramena.

[2] I read pratibhvo, though it should be pratibhuvo.

[3] Could nâsaubadho (C) mean 'there was no murderer of any one?'

hermitages, wells, cisterns, lakes, and groves, having beheld heaven as it were visible before their eyes.

13. The people, delivered from famine, fear, and sickness, dwelt happily as in heaven; and in mutual contentment husband transgressed not against wife, nor wife against husband.

14. None pursued love for mere sensual pleasure; none hoarded wealth for the sake of desires; none practised religious duties for the sake of gaining wealth; none injured living beings for the sake of religious duty.

15. On every side theft and its kindred vices disappeared; his own dominion was in peace and at rest from foreign interference[1]; prosperity and plenty belonged to him, and the cities in his realm were (healthy) like the forests[2].

16. When that son was born it was in that monarch's kingdom as in the reign of Manu the son of the Sun,—gladness went everywhere and evil perished; right blazed abroad and sin was still.

17. Since at the birth of this son of the king such a universal accomplishment of all objects took place, the king in consequence caused the prince's name to be Sarvârthasiddha[3].

18. But the queen Mâyâ, having seen the great glory of her new-born son, like some *Ri*shi of the

---

[1] The Tibetan seems to have read para*s*okamuktam for para*k*akramuktam.

[2] Cf. VIII, 13. If we read ara*n*yasya we must translate these lines, 'the cities in his kingdom seemed part of the forest champaign.' This line appears to be untranslated in the Tibetan.

[3] He by whom all objects are accomplished.

gods, could not sustain the joy which it brought; and that she might not die she went to heaven.

19. Then the queen's sister, with an influence like a mother's, undistinguished from the real mother in her affection or tenderness, brought up as her own son the young prince who was like the offspring of the gods.

20. Then like the young sun on the eastern mountain or the fire when fanned by the wind, the prince gradually grew in all due perfection, like the moon in the fortnight of brightness.

21. Then they brought him as presents from the houses of his friends costly unguents of sandalwood, and strings of gems exactly like wreaths of plants, and little golden carriages yoked with deer;

22. Ornaments also suitable to his age, and elephants, deer, and horses made of gold[1], carriages and oxen decked with rich garments, and carts[2] gay with silver and gold.

23. Thus indulged with all sorts of such objects to please the senses as were suitable to his years,— child as he was, he behaved not like a child in gravity, purity, wisdom, and dignity.

24. When he had passed the period of childhood and reached that of middle youth, the young prince learned in a few days the various sciences suitable to his race, which generally took many years to master.

25. But having heard before from the great seer Asita his destined future which was to embrace

---

[1] Cf. Satyavat's toy horses in Mahâbh. III, 16670.
[2] Gamtrî has this meaning in the Amarakosha and Hemakandra.

transcendental happiness, the anxious care[1] of the king of the present Sâkya race turned the prince to sensual pleasures.

26. Then he sought for him from a family of unblemished moral excellence a bride possessed of beauty, modesty, and gentle bearing, of wide-spread glory, Yasodharâ by name, having a name well worthy of her, a very goddess of good fortune.

27. Then after that the prince, beloved of the king his father, he who was like Sanatkumâra, rejoiced in the society of that Sâkya princess as the thousand-eyed (Indra) rejoiced with his bride Sakî.

28. 'He might perchance see some inauspicious sight which could disturb his mind,'—thus reflecting the king had a dwelling prepared for him apart from the busy press in the recesses of the palace.

29. Then he spent his time in those royal apartments, furnished with the delights proper for every season, gaily decorated like heavenly chariots upon the earth, and bright like the clouds of autumn, amidst the splendid musical concerts of singing-women.

30. With the softly-sounding tambourines beaten by the tips of the women's hands, and ornamented with golden rims, and with the dances which were like the dances of the heavenly nymphs, that palace shone like Mount Kailâsa.

31. There the women delighted him with their soft voices, their beautiful pearl-garlands, their playful intoxication, their sweet laughter, and their stolen glances concealed by their brows.

---

[1] The last pâda seems spurious as it is only found in C. I have tried to make some sense by reading buddhih for vriddhih.

32. Borne in the arms of these women well-skilled in the ways of love, and reckless in the pursuit of pleasure, he fell from the roof of a pavilion and yet reached not the ground, like a holy sage stepping from a heavenly chariot.

33. Meanwhile the king for the sake of ensuring his son's prosperity and stirred in heart by the destiny which had been predicted for him, delighted himself in perfect calm, ceased from all evil, practised all self-restraint, and rewarded the good.

34. He turned to no sensual pleasures like one wanting in self-control; he felt no violent delight in any state of birth[1]; he subdued by firmness the restless horses of the senses; and he surpassed his kindred and citizens by his virtues.

35. He sought not learning to vex another; such knowledge as was beneficent, that only he studied; he wished well to all mankind as much as to his own subjects.

36. He worshipped also duly the brilliant (Agni) that tutelary god of the Aṅgirasas, for his son's long life; and he offered oblations in a large fire, and gave gold[2] and cows to the Brahmans.

37. He bathed to purify his body and mind with the waters of holy places and of holy feelings; and at the same time he drank the soma-juice as enjoined by the Veda, and the heartfelt self-produced happiness of perfect calm.

38. He only spoke what was pleasant and not unprofitable; he discoursed about what was true and not ill-natured; he could not speak even to himself

---

[1] Can ganani mean mâtrigrâma?
[2] Or pearls? (krisana.)

for very shame a false pleasant thing or a harsh truth.

39. In things which required to be done, whether they were pleasant or disagreeable, he found no reason either for desire or dislike; he pursued the advantageous which could be attained without litigation[1]; he did not so highly value sacrifice.

40. When a suppliant came to him with a petition, he at once hastened to quench his thirst with the water sprinkled on his gift[2]; and without fighting, by the battle-axe of his demeanour he smote down the arrogant armed with[3] double pride.

41. Thus he took away the one, and protected the seven; he abandoned the seven and kept the five; he obtained the set of three and learned the set of three; he understood the two and abandoned the two[4].

42. Guilty persons, even though he had sentenced them to death, he did not cause to be killed nor even looked on them with anger; he bound them with gentle words and with the reform produced in their character,—even their release was accompanied by no inflicted injury.

43. He performed great religious vows prescribed by ancient seers; he threw aside hostile feelings long cherished; he acquired glory redolent with the fragrance of virtue; he relinquished all passions involving defilement.

---

[1] Professor Max Müller would read vyavahâralabdham, 'all bliss which could be obtained in the lower or vyâvahârika sphere.'

[2] See Colebrooke's Essays, vol. ii, p. 230, note; Manu IX, 168.

[3] Cf. dvi*s*avasam (madam), Rig-veda IX, 104, 2. Professor Kielhorn would suggest dvi*dd*arpam.

[4] The Tibetan, like the Chinese, gives no help here.

44. He desired not to take his tribute of one-sixth without acting as the guardian of his people[1]; he had no wish to covet another's property; he desired not to mention the wrong-doing of his enemies; nor did he wish to fan wrath in his heart.

45. When the monarch himself was thus employed his servants and citizens followed his example, like the senses of one absorbed in contemplation whose mind is abstracted in profound repose.

46. In course of time to the fair-bosomed Yaso-dharâ,—who was truly glorious in accordance with her name,—there was born from the son of Sud-dhodana a son named Râhula, with a face like the enemy of Râhu[2].

47. Then the king who from regard to the welfare of his race had longed for a son and been exceedingly delighted [at his coming],—as he had rejoiced at the birth of his son, so did he now rejoice at the birth of his grandson.

48. 'O how can I feel that love which my son feels for my grandson?' Thus thinking in his joy he at the due time attended to every enjoined rite like one who fondly loves his son and is about to rise to heaven.

49. Standing in the paths of the pre-eminent kings who flourished in primaeval ages, he practised austerities without laying aside his white garments, and he offered in sacrifice only those things which involved no injury to living creatures.

50. He of holy deeds shone forth gloriously, in

---

[1] Cf. Indische Sprüche, 568 (2nd ed.).
[2] I.e. the sun or the moon, as eclipsed by the demon Râhu.

the splendour of royalty and the splendour of penances, conspicuous by his family and his own conduct and wisdom, and desirous to diffuse brightness like the sun.

51. Having offered worship, he whose own glory was secure muttered repetitions of Vedic texts to Svayambhû for the safety of his son, and performed various ceremonies hard to be accomplished, like the god Ka in the first aeon wishing to create living beings.

52. He laid aside weapons and pondered the *S*âstra, he practised perfect calm and underwent various observances, like a hermit he refused all objects of sense, he viewed all his kingdoms[1] like a father.

53. He endured the kingdom for the sake of his son, his son for his family, his family for fame, fame for heaven, heaven for the soul,—he only desired the soul's continuance for the sake of duty.

54. Thus did he practise the various observances as followed by the pious and established from revelation,—ever asking himself, 'now that he has seen the face of his son, how may my son be stopped from going to the forest?'

55. The prudent[2] kings of the earth, who wish to guard their prosperity, watch over their sons in the world; but this king, though loving religion, kept his son from religion and set him free towards all objects of pleasure.

---

[1] Vishayâ*h* seems used here in two senses, 'kingdoms' and 'objects of sense.'

[2] Lit. 'self-possessed,' âtmasa*m*sthâ*h*. Or should we read âtmasa*m*sthâm, 'wishing to keep their prosperity their own?'

56. But all Bodhisattvas, those beings of pre-eminent nature, after knowing the flavour of worldly enjoyments, have departed to the forest as soon as a son is born to them; therefore he too, though he had accomplished all his previous destiny, even when the (final) motive had begun to germinate, still went on pursuing worldly pleasure up to the time of attaining the supreme wisdom.

BOOK III.

1. On a certain day he heard of the forests carpeted with tender grass, with their trees resounding with the kokilas, adorned with lotus-ponds, and which had been all bound up in the cold season.

2. Having heard of the delightful appearance of the city groves beloved by the women, he resolved to go out of doors, like an elephant long shut up in a house.

3. The king, having learned the character of the wish thus expressed by his son, ordered a pleasure-party to be prepared, worthy of his own affection and his son's beauty and youth.

4. He prohibited the encounter of any afflicted common person in the highroad; 'heaven forbid that the prince with his tender nature should even imagine himself to be distressed.'

5. Then having removed out of the way with the greatest gentleness all those who had mutilated limbs or maimed senses, the decrepit and the sick and all squalid beggars, they made the highway assume its perfect beauty.

6. Along this road thus made beautiful, the fortunate prince with his well-trained attendants came down one day at a proper time from the roof of the palace and went to visit the king by his leave.

7. Then the king, with tears rising to his eyes,

having smelt his son's head[1] and long gazed upon him, gave him his permission, saying, 'Go;' but in his heart through affection he could not let him depart.

8. He then mounted a golden chariot, adorned with reins bright like flashing lightning[2], and yoked with four gentle horses, all wearing golden trappings.

9. With a worthy retinue he entered the road which was strewn with heaps of gleaming flowers, with garlands suspended and banners waving, like the moon with its asterism entering the sky.

10. Slowly, slowly he passed along the highway, watched on every side by the citizens, and be-showered by their eyes opened wide with curiosity like blue lotuses.

11. Some praised him for his gentle disposition, others hailed him for his glorious appearance, others eulogised his beauty from his fine countenance and desired for him length of days.

12. Hump-backed men coming out from the great families, and troops of foresters and dwarfs[3], and women coming out from the meaner houses bowed down like the banners of some procession of the gods.

13. [4] 'Hearing the news, 'the prince is going out,' from the attendants of the female apartments, the women hastened to the roofs of the different mansions, having obtained the leave of their lords.

---

[1] Cf. Wilson, Hindu Drama, vol. ii, p. 45, note.

[2] Raśmi may mean 'rays.' For akliva cf. Soph. Philoct. 1455, ἄρσην.

[3] These are all mentioned in the Sâhitya-darpana among the attendants in a seraglio (§ 81).

[4] With this description cf. Raghuv. VII, 5-12; Kâdambarî, p. 74.

14. Hindered by the strings of their girdles which had slipped down, with their eyes bewildered as just awakened from sleep, and with their ornaments hastily put on in the stir of the news, and filled with curiosity, they crowded round;

15. Frightening the flocks of birds which lived in the houses, with the noise of their girdles and the jingling of their anklets which resounded on the staircases and roofs of the mansions, and mutually reproaching one another for their hurry.

16. Some of these women, even in their haste as they rushed longing to see, were delayed in their going by the weight of their hips and full bosoms.

17. Another, though well able to go herself, checked her pace and forbore to run, hiding with shame her ornaments hitherto worn only in seclusion, and now too boldly displayed.

18. There they were restlessly swaying about in the windows, crowded together in the mutual press, with their earrings polished by the continual collision and their ornaments all jingling.

19. The lotus-like faces of the women gleamed while they looked out from the windows with their earrings coming into mutual proximity[1], as if they were real lotuses fastened upon the houses.

20. With the palaces all alive with crowds of damsels, every aperture thrown open in eager curiosity, the magnificent city appeared on every side like heaven with its divine chariots thronged with celestial nymphs.

21. The faces of the beautiful women shone like lotuses wreathed in garlands, while through the

---

[1] Parasparopâsita?

narrowness of the windows their earrings were transferred to each other's cheeks.

22. Gazing down upon the prince in the road, the women appeared as if longing to fall to the earth; gazing up to him with upturned faces, the men seemed as if longing to rise to heaven [1].

23. Beholding the king's son thus radiant in his beauty and glory, those women softly whispered, ' happy is his wife,' with pure minds and from no baser feeling.

24. 'He with the long sturdy arms, who stands in his beauty like the flower-armed god visibly present, will leave his royal pomp and devote himself to religion,' thus thinking, full of kindly feelings towards him, they all offered reverence.

25. Beholding for the first time that high-road thus crowded with respectful citizens, all dressed in white sedate garments, the prince for a while did feel a little pleasure and thought that it seemed to promise a revival of his youth.

26. But then the gods, dwelling in pure abodes [2], having beheld that city thus rejoicing like heaven itself, created an old man to walk along on purpose to stir the heart of the king's son.

27. The prince having beheld him thus overcome with decrepitude and different in form from other men, with his gaze intently fixed on him, thus addressed his driver [3] with simple confidence:

28. 'Who is this man that has come here, O charioteer, with white hair and his hand resting on a staff, his eyes hidden beneath his brows, his

---

[1] Cf. Uhland's 'Das Schloss am meere.'
[2] *S*uddhâdhivâsâ*h*.   [3] Cf. sa*m*gâhako in Pâli.

limbs bent down and hanging loose,—is this a change produced in him or his natural state or an accident?'

29. Thus addressed, the charioteer revealed to the king's son the secret that should have been kept so carefully, thinking no harm in his simplicity, for those same gods had bewildered his mind:

30. 'That is old age by which he is broken down,—the ravisher of beauty, the ruin of vigour, the cause of sorrow, the destruction of delights, the bane of memories, the enemy of the senses.

31. 'He too once drank milk in his childhood, and in course of time he learned to grope on the ground; having step by step become a vigorous youth, he has step by step in the same way reached old age.'

32. Being thus addressed, the prince, starting a little, spoke these words to the charioteer, 'What! will this evil come to me also?' and to him again spoke the charioteer:

33. 'It will come without doubt by the force of time through multitude of years even to my long-lived lord; all the world knows thus that old age will destroy their comeliness and they are content to have it so.'

34. Then he, the great-souled one, who had his mind purified by the impressions of former good actions, who possessed a store of merits accumulated through many preceding aeons, was deeply agitated when he heard of old age, like a bull who has heard the crash of a thunderbolt close by.

35. Drawing a long sigh and shaking his head, and fixing his eyes on that decrepit old man, and looking round on that exultant multitude he then uttered these distressed words:

36. 'Old age thus strikes down all alike, our memory, comeliness, and valour; and yet the world is not disturbed, even when it sees such a fate visibly impending.

37. 'Since such is our condition, O charioteer, turn back the horses,—go quickly home; how can I rejoice in the pleasure-garden, when the thoughts arising from old age overpower me?'

38. Then the charioteer at the command of the king's son turned the chariot back, and the prince lost in thought entered even that royal palace as if it were empty.

39. But when he found no happiness even there, as he continually kept reflecting, 'old age, old age,' then once more, with the permission of the king, he went out with the same arrangement as before.

40. Then the same deities created another man with his body all afflicted by disease; and on seeing him the son of *S*uddhodana addressed the charioteer, having his gaze fixed on the man:

41. 'Yonder man with a swollen belly, his whole frame shaking as he pants, his arms and shoulders hanging loose, his body all pale and thin, uttering plaintively the word "mother," when he embraces a stranger,—who, pray, is this?'

42. Then his charioteer answered, 'Gentle Sir, it is a very great affliction called sickness, that has grown up, caused by the inflammation of the (three) humours, which has made even this strong man[1] no longer master of himself.'

43. Then the prince again addressed him, looking upon the man compassionately, ' Is this evil peculiar

---

[1] *S*akro*pi.

to him or are all beings alike threatened by sickness?'

44. Then the charioteer answered, 'O prince, this evil is common to all; thus pressed round by diseases men run to pleasure, though racked with pain[1].'

45. Having heard this account, his mind deeply distressed, he trembled like the moon reflected in the waves of water; and full of sorrow he uttered these words in a low voice:

46. 'Even while they see all this calamity of diseases mankind can yet feel tranquillity; alas for the scattered intelligence of men who can smile when still not free from the terrors of disease!

47. 'Let the chariot, O charioteer, be turned back from going outside, let it return straight to the king's palace; having heard this alarm of disease, my mind shrinks into itself, repelled from pleasures.'.

48. Then having turned back, with all joy departed, he entered his home, absorbed in thought; and having seen him thus return a second time, the king himself entered the city.

49. Having heard the occasion of the prince's return he felt himself as deserted by him, and, although unused to severe punishment, even when displeased, he rebuked him whose duty it was to see that the road was clear.

50. And once more he arranged for his son all kinds of worldly enjoyments to their highest point; imploring in his heart, 'Would that he might not be able to forsake us, even though rendered unable only through the restlessness of his senses[2].'

---

[1] Ru*g*âturo. [The Tibetan seems to have read ru*g*âm*t*are,— nad thar-phyin-na, 'having come to the end of illness.' H.W.]

[2] I would read api nâma sakto—.

51. But when in the women's apartments his son found no pleasure in the several objects of the senses, sweet sounds and the rest, he gave orders for another progress outside, thinking to himself[1], 'It may create a diversion of sentiment[2].'

52. And in his affection pondering on the condition of his son, never thinking of any ills that might come from his haste, he ordered the best singing-women to be in attendance, as well-skilled in all the soft arts that can please.

53. Then the royal road being specially adorned and guarded, the king once more made the prince go out, having ordered the charioteer and chariot to proceed in a contrary direction (to the previous one).

54. But as the king's son was thus going on his way, the very same deities created a dead man, and only the charioteer and the prince, and none else, beheld him as he was carried dead along the road.

55. Then spoke the prince to the charioteer, 'Who is this borne by four men, followed by mournful companions, who is bewailed, adorned but no longer breathing[3]?'

56. Then the driver,—having his mind overpowered by the gods who possess pure minds and pure dwellings,—himself knowing the truth, uttered to his lord this truth also which was not to be told:

57. 'This is some poor man who, bereft of his intellect, senses, vital airs and qualities, lying asleep

---

[1] I would read manyamānaḥ.
[2] A technical term in rhetoric. Cf. Sâhitya Darp. § 220.
[3] I would read aśvâsy avarudyate.

and unconscious, like mere wood or straw, is abandoned alike by friends and enemies after they have carefully swathed and guarded him.'

58. Having heard these words of the charioteer he was somewhat startled and said to him, 'Is this an accident peculiar to him alone, or is such the end of all living creatures?'

59. Then the charioteer replied to him, 'This is the final end of all living creatures; be it a mean man, a man of middle state, or a noble, destruction is fixed to all in this world.'

60. Then the king's son, sedate though he was, as soon as he heard of death, immediately sank down overwhelmed, and pressing the end of the chariot-pole with his shoulder spoke with a loud voice,

61. 'Is this end appointed to all creatures, and yet the world throws off all fear and is infatuated! Hard indeed, I think, must the hearts of men be, who can be self-composed in such a road.

62. 'Therefore, O charioteer, turn back our chariot, this is no time or place for a pleasure-excursion; how can a rational being, who knows what destruction is, stay heedless here, in the hour of calamity[1]?'

63. Even when the prince thus spoke to him, the charioteer did not turn the chariot back; but at his peremptorily reiterated command he retired to the forest Padmakha*nd*a.

64. There he beheld that lovely forest like Nandana itself, full of young trees in flower, with intoxicated kokilas wandering joyously about, and

---

[1] The Tibetan has ñam thag dus-su, 'at the time of oppression (as by misfortune).' Does this imply a reading ârtti-kâle?

with its bright lakes gay with lotuses and well-furnished with watering-places [1].

65. The king's son was perforce carried away to that wood filled with troops of beautiful women, just as if some devotee who had newly taken his vow were carried off, feeling weak to withstand temptation, to the palace of the monarch of Alakâ [2], gay with the dancing of the loveliest heavenly nymphs.

---

[1] Sc. for cattle, cf. Mahâbh. XII, 9270 (in the text read -dîrghikam).

[2] Kuvera.

BOOK IV.

1. Then from that city-garden, with their eyes restless in excitement, the women went out to meet the prince as a newly-arrived bridegroom;

2. And when they came up to him, their eyes wide open in wonder, they performed their due homage with hands folded like a lotus-calyx.

3. Then they stood surrounding him, their minds overpowered by passion, as if they were drinking him in with their eyes motionless and blossoming wide with love.

4. Some of the women verily thought that he was Kâma incarnate,—decorated as he was with his brilliant signs as with connate ornaments.

5. Others thought from his gentleness and majesty that it was the moon with its ambrosial beams as it were visibly come down to the earth.

6. Others, smitten by his beauty, yawned[1] as if to swallow him, and fixing their eyes on each other, softly sighed.

7. Thus the women only looked upon him, simply gazing with their eyes,—they spoke not, nor did they smile, controlled by his power.

8. But having seen them thus listless, bewildered in their love, the wise son of the family priest, Udâyin, thus addressed them:

9. 'Ye are all skilled in all the graceful arts,

---

[1] Cf. Sâhitya Darp. § 155, 13.

proficients in understanding the language of amorous sentiments, possessed of beauty and gracefulness, thorough masters in your own styles.

10. 'With these graces of yours ye may embellish even the Northern Kurus, yea, even the dances[1] of Kuvera, much more this little earth.

11. 'Ye are able to move even sages who have lost all their desires, and to ensnare even the gods who are charmed by heavenly nymphs.

12. 'By your skill in expressing the heart's feelings, by your coquetry, your grace, and your perfect beauty, ye are able to enrapture even women, how much more easily men.

13. 'You thus skilled as ye are, each set[2] in her own proper sphere,—such as this is your power,—I am not satisfied with your simplicity [when you profess to find him beyond your reach].

14. 'This timid action of yours would be fit for new brides, their eyes closed through shame,—or it might be a blandishment worthy even of the wives of the cowherds[3].

15. 'What though this hero be great by his exalted glory, yet "great is the might of women," let this be your firm resolve.

16. 'In olden time a great seer, hard to be conquered even by the gods, was spurned by a harlot, the beauty of Kâsi, planting her feet upon him.

17. 'The Bhikshu Manthâlagautama was also formerly spurned by Bâlamukhyâ with her leg, and

---

[1] Professor Bühler suggests kâkri*d*am, cf. *s*loka 28.
[2] I read niyuktânâm for viyuktânâm.
[3] Is this a reference to Kr*ish*na's story? but cf. Weber, Ind. Antiquary, vol. v, p. 254.

wishing to please her he carried out dead bodies for her sake to be buried.

18. 'And a woman low in standing and caste fascinated the great seer Gautama, though a master of long penances and old in years.

19. 'So *S*ântâ[1] by her various wiles captivated and subdued the sage's son *R*ishya*sr*iṅga, unskilled in women's ways.

20. 'And the great seer Vi*s*vâmitra, though plunged in a profound penance[2], was carried captive for ten years in the forests by the nymph Gh*r*itâ*k*î[3].

21. 'Many such seers as these have women brought to shame,—how much more then a delicate prince in the first flower of his age?

22. 'This being so, boldly put forth your efforts that the prosperity of the king's family may not be turned away from him.

23. 'Ordinary women captivate similar lovers; but they are truly women who subdue the natures of high and low.'

24. Having heard these words of Udâyin these women as stung to the heart rose even above themselves for the conquest of the prince.

25. With their brows, their glances, their coquetries, their smiles, their delicate movements, they made all sorts of significant gestures like women utterly terrified.

26. But they soon regained their confidence[4] through the command of the king and the gentle temperament of the prince, and through the power of intoxication and of love.

---

[1] Râmây. I, 10 (Schleg. ed.).   [2] I would read mahat tapa*h*.
[3] Râmây. IV, 35.   [4] Lit. 'dispelled their want of confidence.'

27. Then surrounded by troops of women the prince wandered in the wood like an elephant in the forests of Himavat accompanied by a herd of females.

28. Attended by the women he shone in that pleasant grove, as the sun surrounded by Apsarasas in his royal garden.

29. There some of them, urged by passion, pressed him with their full firm bosoms in gentle collisions.

30. Another violently embraced him after making a pretended stumble,—leaning on him with her shoulders drooping down, and with her gentle creeper-like arms dependent.

31. Another with her mouth smelling of spirituous liquor, her lower lip red like copper, whispered in his ear, 'Let my secret be heard.'

32. Another, all wet with unguents, as if giving him her command, clasped his hand eagerly and said, 'Perform thy rites of adoration here.'

33. Another, with her blue garments continually slipping down in pretended intoxication, stood conspicuous with her tongue visible like the night with its lightning flashing.

34. Others, with their golden zones tinkling, wandered about here and there, showing to him their hips veiled with thin cloth.

35. Others leaned, holding a mango-bough in full flower, displaying their bosoms like golden jars.

36. Another, coming from a lotus-bed, carrying lotuses and with eyes like lotuses, stood like the lotus-goddess Padmâ, by the side of that lotus-faced prince.

37. Another sang a sweet song easily understood and with the proper gesticulations, rousing

him, self-subdued though he was, by her glances, as saying, 'O how thou art deluded!'

38. Another, having armed herself[1] with her bright face, with its brow-bow drawn to its full, imitated his action, as playing the hero.

39. Another, with beautiful full bosoms, and having her earrings waving in the wind[2], laughed loudly at him, as if saying, 'Catch me, sir, if you can!'

40. Some, as he was going away, bound him with strings of garlands,—others punished him with words like an elephant-driver's hook, gentle yet reproachful.

41. Another, wishing to argue with him, seizing a mango-spray, asked, all bewildered with passion, 'This flower, whose is it?'

42. Another, assuming a gait and attitude like those of a man, said to him, 'Thou who art conquered by women, go and conquer this earth!'

43. Then another with rolling eyes, smelling a blue lotus, thus addressed the prince with words slightly indistinct in her excitement,

44. 'See, my lord, this mango covered with its honey-scented flowers, where the kokila sings, as if imprisoned in a golden cage.

45. 'Come and see this a*s*oka tree, which augments lovers' sorrows,—where the bees make a noise as if they were scorched by fire.

46. 'Come and see this tilaka tree, embraced by a slender mango-branch, like a man in a white garment by a woman decked with yellow unguents.

47. 'Behold this kuruvaka in flower, bright like

---

[1] Prâv*ri*tya.   [2] I read vâtâghûr*n*ita.

fresh¹ resin-juice, which bends down as if it felt reproached by the colour of women's nails².

48. 'Come and see this young asoka, covered all over with new shoots, which stands as it were ashamed at the beauty of our hands.

49. 'See this lake surrounded by the sinduvâra shrubs growing on its banks³, like a fair woman reclining, clad in fine white cloth.

50. 'See the imperial power of females,—yonder ruddy-goose in the water goes behind his mate following her like a slave.

51. 'Come and listen to the notes of this intoxicated cuckoo as he sings, while another cuckoo sings as if consenting, wholly without care.

52. 'Would that thine was the intoxication of the birds which the spring produces,—and not the thought of a thinking man, ever pondering how wise he is!'

53. Thus these young women, their souls carried away by love, assailed the prince with all kinds of stratagems.

54. But although thus attacked, he, having his senses guarded by self-control, neither rejoiced nor smiled, thinking anxiously, 'One must die.'

55. Having seen them in their real condition⁴, that best of men pondered with an undisturbed⁵ and stedfast mind.

---

¹ I read nirmuktam, which might mean 'just exuded,' or the whole compound may mean (cf. Kum. Sambh. V, 34) 'like a lip which has given up the use of pinguent.'
² Cf. Vikramorvasî, Act ɪɪ, strî-nakha-pâ*talam kuruvakam.
³ I read tîragaiḥ sinduvârakaiḥ.
⁴ For vasthânam cf. Maitri Upan. (Comm.) VI, 1.
⁵ I would read asamvignena.

56. 'What is it that these women lack[1] that they perceive not that youth is fickle? for this old age will destroy whatever has beauty.

57. 'Verily they do not see any one's plunge into disease, and so dismissing fear, they are joyous in a world which is all pain.

58. 'Evidently they know nothing of death which carries all away; and so at ease and without distress they can sport and laugh.

59. 'What rational being, who knows of old age, death and sickness, could stand[2] or sit down at his ease or sleep, far less laugh?

60. 'But he verily is like one bereft of sense, who, beholding another aged or sick or dead, remains self-possessed and not afflicted.

61. '(So) even when a tree is deprived of its flowers and fruits, or if it is cut down and falls, no other tree sorrows.'

62. Seeing him thus absorbed in contemplation, with his desires estranged from all worldly objects, Udâyin, well skilled in the rules of policy, with kindly feelings addressed him:

63. 'Since I was appointed by the king as a fitting friend for thee, therefore I have a wish to speak to thee in this friendliness of my heart.

64. 'To hinder from what is disadvantageous,—to urge to what is advantageous,—and not to forsake in misfortune,—these are the three marks of a friend.

65. 'If I, after having promised my friendship, were not to heed when thou turnest away from the great end of man, there would be no friendship in me.

---

[1] Kim vinâ.   [2] I would conjecture tish*th*en.

66. 'Therefore I speak as thy friend,—such rudeness as this to women is not befitting for one young in years and graceful in person.

67. 'It is right to woo a woman even by guile,—this is useful both for getting rid of shame and for one's own enjoyment.

68. 'Reverential behaviour and compliance with her wishes are what binds a woman's heart; good qualities truly are a cause of love, and women love respect.

69. 'Wilt thou not then, O large-eyed prince, even if thy heart is unwilling, seek to please them with a courtesy worthy of this beauty of thine?

70. 'Courtesy is the balm of women, courtesy is the best ornament; beauty without courtesy is like a grove without flowers.

71. 'But of what use is courtesy by itself? let it be assisted by the heart's feelings; surely, when worldly objects so hard to attain are in thy grasp, thou wilt not despise them.

72. 'Knowing that pleasure was the best of objects, even the god Pura*m*dara (Indra) wooed in olden time Ahalyâ the wife of the saint Gautama.

73. 'So too Agastya wooed Rohi*nî*, the wife of Soma; and therefore, as *S*ruti saith, a like thing befell Lopâmudrâ[1].

74. 'The great ascetic V*ri*haspati begot Bharadvâga on Mamatâ the daughter of the Maruts, the wife of Autathya[2].

---

[1] Agastya's wife. This seems to refer to Lopâmudrâ's words to her husband in Rig-veda I, 179; cf. also Mahâbh. III, xcvii.

[2] This should be Utathya (cf. Mahâbh. I, civ). Mamatâ had Dîrghatamas by her husband and Bharadvâga by V*ri*haspati. The MSS. read Samatâ.

75. 'The Moon, the best of offerers, begat Budha of divine nature on the spouse of V*ri*haspati as she was offering a libation [1].

76. 'So too in old time Parâsara, overpowered by passion on the bank of the Yamunâ, lay with the maiden Kâlî who was the daughter of the son of the Water (Agni).

77. 'The sage Va*sish*t*h*a through lust begot a son Kapi*ṅ*galâda on Akshamâlâ a despised low-caste woman [2].

78. 'And the seer-king Yayâti, even when the vigour of his prime was gone, sported in the *K*aitraratha forest with the Apsaras Vi*sv*â*k*î.

79. 'And the Kaurava king Pâ*nd*u, though he knew that intercourse with his wife would end in death, yet overcome by the beauty and good qualities of Mâdrî yielded to the pleasures of love.

80. 'And so Karâlaganaka, when he carried off the Brâhman's daughter, incurred loss of caste thereby, but he would not give up his love.

81. 'Great heroes such as these pursued even contemptible desires for the sake of pleasure, how much more so when they are praiseworthy of their kind?

82. 'And yet thou, a young man, possessed of strength and beauty, despisest enjoyments which rightly belong to thee, and to which the whole world is devoted.'

83. Having heard these specious words of his, well-supported by sacred tradition, the prince made reply, in a voice like the thundering of a cloud:

---

[1] She is called Târâ, Vish*n*u Pur. IV, 6.   [2] Manu IX, 23.

84. 'This speech manifesting affection is well-befitting in thee; but I will convince thee as to where thou wrongly judgest me.

85. 'I do not despise worldly objects, I know that all mankind are bound up therein; but remembering that the world is transitory, my mind cannot find pleasure in them.

86. 'Old age, disease, and death—if these three things did not exist, I too should find my enjoyment in the objects that please the mind.

87. 'Yet even though this beauty of women were to remain perpetual, still delight in the pleasures of desire would not be worthy of the wise man.

88. 'But since their beauty will be drunk up by old age, to delight therein through infatuation cannot be a thing approved even by thyself[1].

89. 'He who himself subject to death, disease, and old age, can sport undisturbed with those whose very nature implies death, disease, and old age,— such a man is on a level with birds and beasts.

90. 'And as for what thou sayest as to even those great men having become victims to desire,— do not be bewildered by them, for destruction was also their lot.

91. 'Real greatness is not to be found there, where there is universally destruction, or where there is attachment to earthly objects, or a want of self-control.

92. 'And when thou sayest, "Let one deal with women even by guile," I know nought about guile, even if it be accompanied with courtesy.

93. 'That compliance too with a woman's wishes

---

[1] Or 'even by the soul.'

pleases me not, if truthfulness be not there; if there be not a union with one's whole soul and nature, then "out upon it" say I.

94. 'A soul overpowered by passion, believing in falsehood, carried away by attachment and blind to the faults of its objects,—what is there in it worth being deceived?

95. 'And if the victims of passion do deceive one another,—are not men unfit for women to look at and women for men?

96. 'Since then these things are so, thou surely wouldest not lead me astray into ignoble pleasures, —me afflicted by sorrow, and subject to old age and death?

97. 'Ah! thy mind must be very firm and strong, if thou canst find substance in the transitory pleasures of sense; even in the midst of violent alarm thou canst cling to worldly objects, when thou seest all created beings in the road of death.

98. 'But I am fearful and exceedingly bewildered, as I ponder the terrors of old age, death, and disease; I can find no peace, no self-command, much less can I find pleasure, while I see the world as it were ablaze with fire.

99. 'If desire arises in the heart of the man, who knows that death is certain,—I think that his soul must be made of iron, who restrains it in this great terror and does not weep.'

100. Then the prince uttered a discourse full of resolve and abolishing the objects of desire; and the lord of day, whose orb is the worthy centre of human eyes, departed to the Western Mountain.

101. And the women, having worn their garlands and ornaments in vain, with their graceful arts and

endearments all fruitless, concealing their love deep in their hearts¹, returned to the city with broken hopes.

102. Having thus seen the beauty² of the troop of women who had gone out to the city-garden, now withdrawn in the evening,—the prince, pondering the transitoriness which envelopes all things, entered his dwelling.

103. Then the king, when he heard how his mind turned away from all objects of sense, could not lie down all that night, like an elephant with an arrow in its heart; but wearied in all sorts of consultation, he and his ministers could find no other means beside these (despised) pleasures to restrain his son's purpose.

---

[1] Reading sva eva bhâve from the Tibetan.
[2] Reading *sriyam* for striyam.

BOOK V.

1. He, the son of the *S*âkya king, even though thus tempted by the objects of sense which infatuate others, yielded not to pleasure and felt not delight, like a lion deeply pierced in his heart by a poisoned arrow.

2. Then one day accompanied by some worthy sons of his father's ministers, friends full of varied converse,—with a desire to see the glades of the forest and longing for peace, he went out with the king's permission.

3. Having mounted his good horse Ka*m*thaka, decked with bells and bridle-bit of new gold, with beautiful golden harness and the chowrie waving[1], he went forth like the moon[2] mounted on a comet.

4. Lured by love of the wood and longing for the beauties of the ground[3], he went to a spot near at hand[4] on the forest-outskirts; and there he saw a piece of land being ploughed, with the path of the plough broken like waves on the water.

---

[1] 'The white bushy tail of the Tibet cow, fixed on a gold or ornamented shaft, rose from between the ears of the horse.' Wilson, Hindu Drama, I, p. 200.

[2] The Tibetan has tog-la ljon-dan chu-skyes tog-can, 'like him who has the sign of a tree and water-born (lotus,) (mounted) on a comet,' but with no further explanation. Could this mean the moon as oshadhipati and as kumu e*s*a?

[3] Should we read -gu*n*ek*kh*uh for -gunâk*kh*ah?

[4] Nik*r*ish*t*atarâm; one MS. reads vik*r*ish*t*a-, 'ploughed.'

5. Having beheld the ground in this condition, with its young grass scattered and torn by the plough, and covered with the eggs and young of little insects which were killed, he was filled with deep sorrow as for the slaughter of his own kindred.

6. And beholding the men as they were ploughing, their complexions spoiled by the dust, the sun's rays, and the wind, and their cattle bewildered with the burden of drawing, the most noble one felt extreme compassion.

7. Having alighted from the back of his horse, he went over the ground slowly, overcome with sorrow, —pondering the birth and destruction of the world, he, grieved, exclaimed, 'this is indeed pitiable.'

8. Then desiring to become perfectly lonely in his thoughts, having stopped those friends who were following him, he went to the root of a rose-apple in a solitary spot, which had its beautiful leaves all tremulous (in the wind).

9. There he sat down on the ground covered with leaves [1], and with its young grass bright like lapis lazuli; and, meditating on the origin and destruction of the world, he laid hold of the path that leads to firmness of mind.

10. Having attained to firmness of mind [2], and being forthwith set free from all sorrows such as the desire of worldly objects and the rest, he attained

---

[1] The MSS. add -khoravatyâm, an obscure word, which may be connected with khura or perhaps should be altered to -koravatyâm, i.e. 'covered with sharp-pointed leaves,' or 'covered with leaves and buds.' [The Tibetan has gcan-mar ldan-pai sa-gzhi der-ni de zhugs-te, 'on the pure ground here he sitting.' This might point to sо·tra saukavatyâm. H.W.]

[2] Query, samavâptamanahsthitih for -manâhsthiteh.

the first stage of contemplation, unaffected by sin, calm, and 'argumentative¹.'

11. Having then obtained the highest happiness sprung from deliberation², he next pondered this meditation,—having thoroughly understood in his mind the course of the world:

12. 'It is a miserable thing that mankind, though themselves powerless³ and subject to sickness, old age, and death, yet, blinded by passion and ignorant, look with disgust on another who is afflicted by old age or diseased or dead.

13. 'If I here, being such myself, should feel disgust for another who has such a nature, it would not be worthy or right in me who know this highest duty.'

14. As he thus considered thoroughly these faults of sickness, old age, and death which belong to all living beings, all the joy which he had felt in the activity of his vigour, his youth, and his life, vanished in a moment.

15. He did not rejoice, he did not feel remorse; he suffered no hesitation, indolence, nor sleep; he felt no drawing towards the qualities of desire; he hated not nor scorned another.

16. Thus did this pure passionless meditation grow within the great-souled one; and unobserved by the other men, there crept up a man in a beggar's dress.

17. The king's son asked him a question,—he said to him, 'Tell me, who art thou?' and the other replied, 'Oh bull of men, I, being terrified at birth

---

¹ *S*avitarka, cf. Yoga-sûtras I, 42. (Read anâsrava-.)
² Two syllables are lost in this line. ³ Arasa*h*.

and death, have become an ascetic for the sake of liberation.

18. 'Desiring liberation in a world subject to destruction, I seek that happy indestructible abode,—isolated from mankind, with my thoughts unlike those of others, and with my sinful passions turned away from all objects of sense

19. 'Dwelling anywhere, at the root of a tree, or in an uninhabited house, a mountain or a forest,—I wander without a family and without hope, a beggar ready for any fare, seeking only the highest good.'

20. When he had thus spoken, while the prince was looking on, he suddenly flew up to the sky; it was a heavenly inhabitant who, knowing that the prince's thoughts were other than what his outward form promised, had come to him for the sake of rousing his recollection.

21. When the other was gone like a bird to heaven, the foremost of men was rejoiced and astonished; and having comprehended the meaning of the term dharma[1], he set his mind on the manner of the accomplishment of deliverance.

22. Then like Indra himself, and having tamed his senses,—desiring to return home he mounted his noble steed; and having made him turn back as he looked for his friends, from that moment he sought no more the desired forest.

23. Ever seeking to make an end of old age and death, fixing his thoughts in memory on dwelling in the woods, he entered the city again but with no feelings of longing, like an elephant entering an exercise-ground[2] after roaming in a forest-land.

24. 'Happy truly and blessed is that woman whose

---

[1] Dharmasa*mgñ*âm? [2] Cf. II, 3.

husband is such as thou, O long-eyed prince!' So, on seeing him, the princess exclaimed, folding her hands to welcome him, as he entered the road.

25. He whose voice was deep-sounding like a cloud heard this address and was filled with profound calm; and as he heard the word 'blessed[1]' he fixed his mind on the attainment of Nirvâ*n*a.

26. Then the prince whose form was like the peak of a golden mountain,—whose eye, voice, and arm resembled a bull, a cloud, and an elephant[2],—whose countenance and prowess were like the moon and a lion,—having a longing aroused for something imperishable,—went into his palace.

27. Then stepping like a lion he went towards the king who was attended by his numerous counsellors, like Sanatkumâra in heaven waiting on Indra resplendent in the assembly[3] of the Maruts.

28. Prostrating himself, with folded hands, he addressed him, 'Grant me graciously thy permission, O lord of men,—I wish to become a wandering mendicant for the sake of liberation, since separation is appointed for me.'

29. Having heard his words, the king shook like a tree struck by an elephant, and having seized his folded hands which were like a lotus, he thus addressed him in a voice choked with tears:

30. 'O my son, keep back this thought, it is not the time for thee to betake thyself to dharma; they say that the practice of religion is full of evils in the first period of life when the mind is still fickle.

---

[1] Sc. nirv*ri*ta.

[2] Ga*g*amegharshabhabâhunisvanâksha*h*? So Chinese translation, Beal, st. 356.

[3] I read samitau.

31. 'The mind of the thoughtless ignorant young man whose senses are eager for worldly objects, and who has no power of settled resolution for the hardships of vows of penance, shrinks back from the forest, for it is especially destitute of discrimination.

32. 'It is high time for me to practise religion, O my child of loved qualities[1], leaving my royal glory to thee who art well worthy to be distinguished by it; but thy religion, O firm-striding hero, is to be accomplished by heroism; it would be irreligion if thou wert to leave thine own father.

33. 'Do thou therefore abandon this thy resolution; devote thyself for the present to the duties of a householder; to a man who has enjoyed the pleasures of his prime, it is delightful to enter the penance-forest.'

34. Having heard these words of the king, he made his reply in a voice soft like a sparrow's: 'If thou wilt be my surety, O king, against four contingencies, I will not betake myself to the forest.

35. 'Let not my life be subject to death, and let not disease impair this health of mine; let not old age attack my youth, and let not misfortune destroy my weal.'

36. When his son uttered a speech so hard to be understood, the king of the Sākyas thus replied: 'Abandon this idea bent upon departure; extravagant desires are only ridiculous.'

37. Then he who was firm as Mount Meru addressed his father: 'If this is impossible, then this course of mine is not to be hindered; it is not right to lay hold of one who would escape[2] from a house that is on fire.

---

[1] Or 'lover of religion.' [2] Read nishkramishum.

38. 'As separation is inevitable to the world, but not for Dharma[1], this separation is preferable; will not death sever me helplessly, my objects unattained and myself unsatisfied?'

39. The monarch, having heard this resolve of his son longing for liberation, and having again exclaimed, 'He shall not go,' set guards round him and the highest pleasures.

40. Then having been duly instructed[2] by the counsellors, with all respect and affection, according to the *sâstras*, and being thus forbidden with tears by his father, the prince, sorrowing, entered into his palace.

41. There he was gazed at by his wives with restless eyes, whose faces were kissed by their dangling earrings, and whose bosoms were shaken with their thick-coming sighs,—as by so many young fawns.

42. Bright like a golden mountain, and bewitching the hearts of the noble women, he enraptured their ears, limbs, eyes, and souls by his speech, touch, form, and qualities.

43. When the day was gone, then, shining with his form like the sun, he ascended the palace, as the rising sun ascends Mount Meru, desiring to dispel the darkness by his own splendour.

44. Having ascended, he repaired to a special golden seat decorated with embellishments of diamond, with tall lighted candlesticks ablaze with gold, and its interior filled with the incense of black aloe-wood.

45. Then the noblest of women waited during the

---

[1] This accompanies the soul at death; cf. Manu VIII, 17.

[2] Does this allude to Udâyin? or should we translate it 'being shown the way?'

night on the noblest of men who was like Indra himself, with a concert of musical instruments, as the crowds of heavenly nymphs wait on the son of the Lord of wealth [1] upon the summit of Himavat, white like the moon.

46. But even by those beautiful instruments like heavenly music he was not moved to pleasure or delight; since his desire to go forth from his home to seek the bliss of the highest end was never lulled.

47. Then by the power of the heavenly beings most excellent in self-mortification, the Akanish*th*as, who knew the purpose of his heart, deep sleep was suddenly thrown on that company of women and their limbs and gestures became distorted [2].

48. One was lying there, resting her cheek on her trembling arm; leaving as in anger her lute, though dearly loved, which lay on her side, decorated with gold-leaf.

49. Another shone with her flute clinging to her hand, lying with her white garments fallen from her bosom,—like a river whose banks are smiling with the foam of the water and whose lotuses are covered with a straight line of bees [3].

50. Another was sleeping [4], embracing her drum as a lover, with her two arms tender like the shoot of a young lotus and bearing their bracelets closely linked, blazing with gold.

51. Others, decked with new golden ornaments

---

[1] Sc. Kuvera. I follow Professor Max Müller's suggested reading himava*kkh*irasíva for the MS. himavadgirisíra.

[2] With this description of the sleeping women compare that in the Râmâya*n*a, V, 10.

[3] The bees represent the flute held in the lotus-like hand.

[4] I would read tathâparâ.

and wearing peerless yellow garments, fell down alas! helpless with sleep, like the boughs of the Kar*n*i-kâra broken by an elephant.

52. Another, leaning on the side of a window, with her willow-form bent like a bow, shone as she lay with her beautiful necklace hanging down, like a statue [1] in an archway made by art.

53. The lotus-face of another, bowed down, with the pinguent-lines on her person rubbed by the jewelled earrings, appeared to be a lotus with its stalk bent into a half-circle, and shaken by a duck standing on it [2].

54. Others, lying as they sat, with their limbs oppressed by the weight of their bosoms, shone in their beauty, mutually clasping one another with their twining arms decorated with golden bracelets.

55. And another damsel lay sound asleep, embracing her big lute as if it were a female friend, and rolled it about, while its golden strings trembled, with her own face bright with her shaken earrings.

56. Another lay, with her tabour, . . .

57. Others showed no lustre with their eyes shut, although they were really full-eyed and fair-browed, —like the lotus-beds with their buds closed at the setting of the sun.

58. Another, with her hair loose and dishevelled, and her skirts and ornaments fallen from her loins, lay with her necklace in confusion, like a woman crushed by an elephant and then dropped.

59. Others, helpless and lost to shame, though

---

[1] Sâlabha*m*gikâ?
[2] This is a hard verse, but the woman's face above the bent body seems to be compared to the duck standing on the flower and bending its stalk.

naturally self-possessed and endued with all graces of person, breathed violently as they lay and yawned with their arms distorted and tossed about.

60. Others, with their ornaments and garlands thrown off,—unconscious, with their garments spread out unfastened,—their bright eyes wide open and motionless,—lay without any beauty as if they were dead.

61. Another, with fully-developed limbs, her mouth wide open, her saliva dropping, and her person exposed, lay as though sprawling in intoxication,—she spoke not, but bore every limb distorted.

62. Thus that company of women, lying in different attitudes, according to their disposition and family, bore the aspect of a lake whose lotuses were bent down and broken by the wind.

63. Then having seen these young women thus lying distorted and with uncontrolled gestures,—however excellent their forms and graceful their appearance,—the king's son felt moved with scorn.

64. 'Such is the nature of women, impure and monstrous in the world of living beings; but deceived by dress and ornaments a man becomes infatuated by a woman's attractions.

65. 'If a man would but consider the natural state of women and this change produced in them by sleep, assuredly he would not cherish his folly; but he is smitten from a right will and so succumbs to passion.'

66. Thus to him having recognised that difference there arose a desire to escape in the night; and then the gods, knowing his purpose, caused the door of the palace to fly open.

67. Then he went down from the roof of the

palace, scorning those women who lay thus distorted; and having descended, undauntedly he went out first into the courtyard[1].

68. Having awakened his horse's attendant, the swift *Kha*m*daka, he thus addressed him: 'Bring me quickly my horse Ka*m*thaka[2], I wish to-day to go hence to attain immortality.

69. 'Since such is the firm content which to-day is produced in my heart, and since my determination is settled in calm resolve, and since even in loneliness I seem to possess a guide,—verily the end which I desire is now before me.

70. 'Since abandoning all shame and modesty these women lay before me as they did, and the two doors opened of their own accord, verily the time is come to depart for my true health.'

71. Then, accepting his lord's command, though he knew the purport of the king's injunctions, as being urged by a higher power in his mind, he set himself to bring the horse.

72. Then he brought out for his master that noble steed, his mouth furnished with a golden bit, his back lightly touched by the bed on which he had been lying, and endued with strength, vigour, speed, and swiftness[3];

73. With a long chine, and root of the tail and heel,—gentle, with short hair, back, and ears,—with his back, belly, and sides depressed and elevated,— with broad nostrils, forehead, hips, and breast[4].

74. The broad-chested hero, having embraced him,

---

[1] Cf. Mahâbh. II, 32.
[2] Spelt in the MSS. sometimes Ka*mth*aka, but not always clear.
[3] Read *g*avatvaropapannam for MS. *g*avatvalo-.
[4] Cf. the description in Shakespeare's Venus and Adonis.

and caressing him with his lotus-like hand, ordered him with a gentle-toned voice, as if he were desirous to plunge into the middle of an army:

75. 'Oftentimes have evil enemies been overthrown by the king when mounted on thee; do thou, O best of steeds, so exert thyself that I too may obtain the highest immortality [1].

76. 'Companions are easy to be found in battle or in the happiness obtained by winning worldly objects or in attaining wealth; but companions are hard for a man to find who has fallen into misfortune or when he flies for refuge to Dharma.

77. 'And yet all those who in this world are companions, whether in sinful custom or in seeking for Dharma,—as my inner soul now recognises,—they too are verily sharers in the common aim.

78. 'Since then, when I attain this righteous end, my escape from hence will be for the good of the world,—O best of steeds, by thy speed and energy, strive for thine own good and the good of the world.'

79. Thus having exhorted the best of steeds like a friend to his duty, he, the best of men, longing to go to the forest, wearing a noble form, in brightness like fire [2], mounted the white horse as the sun an autumnal cloud.

80. Then that good steed, avoiding all noises which would sound startling in the dead of night and awaken the household,—all sound of his jaws hushed and his neighing silenced,—went forth, planting his hurrying steps at full speed.

81. With their lotus-like hands, whose fore-arms

---

[1] Yathâvat=yathâ.
[2] Asitagati seems here used like kr*i*sh*n*agati, 'fire.'

were adorned with golden bracelets, the Yakshas, with their bodies bent down, threw lotuses and bore up his hoofs as he rushed in startled haste.

82. The city-roads which were closed with heavy gates and bars, and which could be with difficulty opened[1] even by elephants, flew open of their own accord without noise, as the prince went through.

83. Firm in his resolve and leaving behind without hesitation his father who turned ever towards him[2], and his young son, his affectionate people and his unparalleled magnificence, he then went forth out of his father's city.

84. Then he with his eyes long and like a full-blown lotus, looking back on the city, uttered a sound like a lion, 'Till I have seen the further shore of birth and death I will never again enter the city called after Kapila.'

85. Having heard this his utterance, the troops of the court of the Lord of wealth[3] rejoiced; and the hosts of the gods, triumphing, wished him a successful accomplishment of his purpose.

86. Other heavenly beings with forms bright like fire, knowing that his purpose was hard to fulfil, produced a light on his dewy path like the rays of the moon issuing from the rift of a cloud.

87. But he with his horse like the horse of Indra, the lord of bay horses, hurrying on as if spurred in his mind, went over the leagues full of many conflicting emotions[4],—the sky all the while with its cloud-masses checkered with the light of the dawn.

---

[1] Apâdhriyante MSS., but I read apâvri-.
[2] Abhimukham.
[3] Sc. the Yakshas.
[4] Or perhaps 'six leagues.'

BOOK VI.

1. Then when the sun, the eye of the world, was just risen, he, the noblest of men, beheld the hermitage of the son of Bh*ri*gu,

2. Its deer all asleep in quiet trust, its birds tranquilly resting,—seeing it he too became restful, and he felt as if his end was attained.

3. For the sake of ending his wonder and to show reverence for the penances observed, and as expressing his own conformity therewith [1], he alighted from the back of his horse.

4. Having alighted, he stroked the horse, exclaiming, 'All is saved,' and he spoke well-pleased to *Kha*ṃdaka, bedewing him as it were with tears from his eyes:

5. 'Good friend, thy devotion to me and thy courage of soul have been proved by thy thus following this steed whose speed is like that of Târkshya [2].

6. 'Bent even though I am on other business, I am wholly won in heart by thee,—one who has such a love for his master, and at the same time is able to carry out his wish.

7. 'One can be able without affection, and affectionate though unable; but one like thee, at once affectionate and able, is hard to find in the world.

---

[1] Svâ*m kâ*nuvartitâ*m* raksha*n*. [The Tibetan has the obscure raṅ·gi rjes·su bsruṅ·va la=sva+anu+raksha*n*? H. W.]

[2] An old mythic representation of the sun as a horse.

8. 'I am pleased with this noble action of thine; this feeling is seen towards me, even though I am regardless of conferring rewards.

9. 'Who would not be favourably disposed to one who stands to him as bringing him reward? but even one's own people commonly become mere strangers in a reverse of fortune [1].

10. 'The son is maintained for the sake of the family, the father is honoured for the sake of our own (future) support; the world shows kindness for the sake of hope; there is no such a thing as unselfishness without a motive.

11. 'Why speak many words? in short, thou hast done me a very great kindness; take now my horse and return, I have attained the desired wood.'

12. Thus having spoken, the mighty hero in his desire to show perfect gentleness [2] unloosed his ornaments and gave them to the other, who was deeply grieved.

13. Having taken a brilliant jewel whose effect illumined his diadem, he stood, uttering these words, like the mountain Ma*m*dara with the sun resting on it:

14. 'By thee with this jewel, O *Kha*m*da, having offered him repeated obeisance, the king, with his loving confidence still unshaken, must be enjoined to stay his grief.

15. '"I have entered the ascetic-wood to destroy old age and death,—with no thirst for heaven, with no lack of love nor feeling of anger.

---

[1] *G*anîbhavati may be a quaint expression for para*g*ano bhavati,—this seems the meaning of the Tibetan. Or we might read *g*anyo bhavati.

[2] Ân*ri*samsa (for ânr*i*samsya), see Pâ*n*ini V, 1, 130 ga*n*a.

16. '"Do not think of mourning for me who am thus gone forth from my home; union, however long it may last, in time will come to an end.

17. '"Since separation is certain, therefore is my mind fixed on liberation; how shall there not be repeated severings from one's kindred?

18. '"Do not think of mourning for me who am gone forth to leave sorrow behind; it is the thralls of passion, who are attached to desires, the causes of sorrow, for whom thou shouldst mourn.

19. '"This was the firm persuasion of our predecessors,—I as one departing by a common road am not to be mourned for by my heir.

20. '"At a man's death there are doubtless heirs to his wealth; but heirs to his merit are hard to find on the earth or exist not at all.

21. '"Even though thou sayest, 'He is gone at a wrong time to the wood,'—there is no wrong time for religious duty (dharma), life being fragile as it is.

22. '"Therefore my determination is, 'I must seek my supreme good this very day;' what confidence can there be in life, when death stands as our adversary?"

23. 'Do thou address the king, O friend, with these and such-like words; and do thou use thy efforts so that he may not even remember me.

24. 'Yea, do thou repeat to the king our utter unworthiness; through unworthiness affection is lost, —and where affection is lost, there is no sorrow.'

25. Having heard these words, *Kha*n*da, overwhelmed with grief, made reply with folded hands, his voice choked by tears:

26. 'At this state of mind of thine, causing afflic-

tion to thy kindred, my mind, O my lord, sinks down like an elephant in the mud of a river.

27. 'To whom would not such a determination as this of thine cause tears, even if his heart were of iron,—how much more if it were throbbing with love?

28. 'Where [1] is this delicacy of limb, fit to lie only in a palace,—and where is the ground of the ascetic-forest, covered with the shoots of rough kuśa grass?

29. 'When, on hearing thy resolve, I first brought thee this horse,—it was fate only, O my lord, which made me do it, mastering my will.

30. 'But how could I, O king, by mine own will,—knowing this thy decision,—carry back the horse to the sorrow of Kapilavastu?

31. 'Surely thou wilt not abandon, O hero, that fond old king, so devoted to his son, as a heretic might the true religion?

32. 'And her, thy second mother, worn with the care of bringing thee up,—thou wilt not surely forget her, as an ingrate a benefit?

33. 'Thou wilt not surely abandon thy queen, endowed with all virtues, illustrious for her family, devoted to her husband and with a young son, as a coward the royal dignity within his reach?

34. 'Thou wilt not abandon the young son of Yaśodharâ, worthy of all praise, thou the best of the cherishers of religion and fame, as a dissolute spendthrift his choicest glory?

35. 'Or even if thy mind be resolved to abandon thy kindred and thy kingdom, thou wilt not, O master, abandon me,—thy feet are my only refuge.

---

[1] A common expression (which occurs also in Persian poetry) to imply the incompatibility of two things.

36. 'I cannot go to the city with my soul thus burning, leaving thee behind in the forest as Sumitra[1] left the son of Raghu.

37. 'What will the king say to me, returning to the city without thee? or what shall I say to thy queens by way of telling them good news?

38. 'As for what thou saidst, "thou must repeat my unworthiness to the king"—how shall I speak what is false of thee as of a sage without a fault?

39. 'Or even if I ventured to speak it with a heart ashamed and a tongue cleaving to my mouth, who would think of believing it?

40. 'He who would tell of or believe the fierceness of the moon, might tell of or believe thy faults, O physician of faults.

41. 'Him who is always compassionate and who never fails to feel pity, it ill befits to abandon one who loves;—turn back and have mercy on me.'

42. Having heard these words of *Kha*ṃ*da* overcome with sorrow,—self-possessed with the utmost firmness the best of speakers answered:

43. 'Abandon this distress, *Kha*ṃ*da*, regarding thy separation from me,—change is inevitable in corporeal beings who are subject to different births.

44. 'Even if I through affection were not to abandon my kindred in my desire for liberation, death would still make us helplessly abandon one another.

45. 'She, my mother, by whom I was borne in the womb with great thirst and pains,—where am I now with regard to her, all her efforts fruitless, and where is she with regard to me?

46. 'As birds go to their roosting-tree and then

---

[1] This is the Sumantra of the Râmâya*n*a II, 57.

depart, so the meeting of beings inevitably ends in separation.

47. 'As clouds, having come together, depart asunder again, such I consider the meeting and parting of living things.

48. 'And since this world goes away, each one of us deceiving the other,—it is not right to think anything thine own in a time of union which is a dream.

49. 'Since the trees are parted from the innate colour of their leaves, why should there not still more be the parting of two things which are alien to each other?

50. 'Therefore, since it is so, grieve not, my good friend, but go; or if thy love lingers, then go and afterwards return.

51. 'Say, without reproaching us, to the people in Kapilavastu, "Let your love for him be given up, and hear his resolve.

52. '"Either he will quickly come back, having destroyed old age and death; or else he will himself perish, having failed in his purpose and lost hold of every support."'

53. Having heard his words, Ka*m*thaka, the noblest of steeds, licked his feet with his tongue and dropped hot tears.

54. With his hand whose fingers were united with a membrane and which was marked with the auspicious svastika, and with its middle part curved[1], the prince stroked him and addressed him like a friend:

55. 'Shed not tears, Ka*m*thaka, this thy perfect

---

[1] Professor Kielhorn suggests *k*akra-madhyena, 'with a wheel in its centre,' cf. VIII, 55.

equine nature has been proved,—bear with it, this thy labour will soon have its fruit.'

56. Then seizing the sharp jewelled sword which was in *Kha*m*daka's hand, he resolutely drew out from the sheath the blade decked with golden ornaments, like a serpent from its hole.

57. Having drawn it forth, dark blue like a blue lotus petal, he cut his decorated tiara and his hair, and he tossed it with its scattered muslin into the air as a grey goose into a lake.

58. And the heavenly beings, with a longing to worship it, seized it respectfully as it was thrown up; and the divine hosts paid it due adoration in heaven with celestial honours.

59. Having thus divorced his ornaments and banished all royal magnificence from his head, and seeing his muslin floating away like a golden goose, the stedfast prince desired a sylvan dress.

60. Then a celestial being, wearing the form of a hunter, pure in heart, knowing his thoughts, approached near him in dark-red garments; and the son of the *S*âkya king thus addressed him:

61. 'Thy red garments are auspicious, the sign of a saint; but this destructive bow is not befitting; therefore, my good friend, if there is no strong preference in the matter, do thou give me that dress and take this of mine.'

62. The hunter replied, 'It has given me my desire [1], O giver of desires, as by this I have inspired

---

[1] I have taken ârât as from â + râ, but Professor Kielhorn suggests that it might mean 'near.' 'Although in this dress I make the deer come confidently close to me and then kill them, yet take it if you want it.' [The Tibetan seems to have read kâmasârât,—₀dod-pa sñin-po las, 'from essence of desire.' H. W.]

animals with confidence and then killed them; but if thou hast need of it, O thou who art like Indra, accept it at once and give me the white dress.'

63. With extreme joy he then took that sylvan dress and gave away the linen one; and the hunter, assuming his heavenly form, having taken the white garment, went to heaven.

64. Then the prince and the attendant of the horse were filled with wonder as he was thus going, and forthwith they paid great honour anew to that sylvan dress.

65. Then the great-souled one, having dismissed the weeping *Kha*mda, and wearing his fame veiled by the sign of the red garment, went towards the hermitage, like the king of mountains wrapped in an evening cloud.

66. While his master, thus regardless of his kingdom, was going to the ascetic-wood in mean garments, the groom, tossing up his arms, wailed bitterly and fell on the ground.

67. Having looked again he wept aloud, and embraced the horse Ka*m*thaka with his arms; and then, hopeless and repeatedly lamenting, he went in body to the city, not in soul.

68. Sometimes he pondered, sometimes he lamented, sometimes he stumbled, and sometimes he fell; and so going along, wretched through his devoted attachment, he performed all kinds of actions in the road without conscious will.

BOOK VII.

1. Then having left the weeping tear-faced *Khaṃda*,—indifferent to all things in his longing for the forest, he by whom all objects are accomplished, overpowering the place by his beauty, entered that hermitage as if it were fully blessed.

2. He the prince with a gait like the lion's, having entered that arena of deer, himself like a deer,—by the beauty of his person, even though bereft of his magnificence, attracted the eyes of all the dwellers in the hermitage.

3. The drivers of wheeled carriages also, with their wives, stood still in curiosity, holding the yokes in their hands,—they gazed on him who was like Indra, and moved not, standing like their beasts of burden with their heads half bent down.

4. And the Brâhmans who had gone outside for the sake of fuel, having come with their hands full of fuel, flowers, and kuśa grass,—pre-eminent as they were in penances, and proficients in wisdom, went to see him, and went not to their cells.

5. Delighted the peacocks uttered their cries, as if they had seen a dark-blue cloud rising up; and leaving the young grass and coming forward, the deer with restless eyes and the ascetics who grazed like deer[1] stood still.

---

[1] A form of ascetic observance, see Mahâbh. I, 3644; V, 4072. Cf. infra, śloka 15.

6. Beholding him, the lamp of the race of Ikshvâku, shining like the rising sun,—even though their milking was over, being filled with joy, the oblation-giving cows poured forth their milk.

7. 'It is one of the eight Vasus or one of the two Asvins, descended here,'—these words arose, uttered aloud by the sages in their astonishment at seeing him.

8. Like a second form of the lord of the gods[1], like the personified glory of the universe, he lighted up the entire wood like the sun come down of his own accord.

9. Then he, being duly honoured and invited to enter by those dwellers in the hermitage, paid his homage to the saints, with a voice like a cloud in the rainy season[2].

10. He, the wise one, longing for liberation, traversed that hermitage filled with the holy company desirous of heaven,—gazing at their strange penances.

11. He, the gentle one, having seen the different kinds of penance practised by the ascetics in that sacred grove,—desiring to know the truth, thus addressed one of the ascetics who was following him:

12. 'Since this to-day is my first sight of a hermitage I do not understand this rule of penance; therefore will your honour kindly explain to me what resolve possesses each one of you.'

13. Then the Brâhman well-versed in penance told in order to that bull of the Sâkyas, a very bull in prowess, all the various kinds of penance and the fruit thereof.

---

[1] Lekharshabha is a rare name of Indra.
[2] A conjectural reading.

14. 'Uncultivated food, growing out of the water, leaves, water, and roots and fruits,—this is the fare of the saints according to the sacred texts; but the different alternatives of penance vary.

15. 'Some live like the birds on gleaned corn, others graze on grass like the deer, others live on air with the snakes, as if turned into ant-hills[1].

16. 'Others win their nourishment with great effort from stones, others eat corn ground with their own teeth; some, having boiled for others, dress for themselves what may chance to be left.

17. 'Others, with their tufts of matted hair continually wet with water, twice offer oblations to Agni with hymns; others plunging like fishes into the water dwell there with their bodies scratched by tortoises.

18. 'By such penances endured for a time,—by the higher they attain heaven, by the lower the world of men; by the path of pain they eventually dwell in happiness,—pain, they say, is the root of merit.'

19. The king's son, having heard this speech of the ascetic, even though he saw no lofty truth in it[2], was not content, but gently uttered these thoughts to himself:

20. 'The penance is full of pain and of many kinds, and the fruit of the penance is mainly heaven at its best, and all the worlds are subject to change; verily the labour of the hermitages is spent for but little gain.

---

[1] Cf. the legend of the princess Sukanyâ, given in Wilson's note, Hindu Drama, I, p. 263.

[2] Cf. Beal, 517 (or perhaps 'though he had not himself yet attained the highest truth').

21. 'Those who abandoning wealth, kindred, and worldly objects, undertake vows for the sake of heaven,—they, when parted, only wish to go to a still greater wood of their own again [1].

22. 'He who by all these bodily toils which are called penances, seeks a sphere of action for the sake of desire,—not examining the inherent evils of mundane existence, he only seeks pain by pain.

23. 'There is ever to living creatures fear from death, and they with all their efforts seek to be born again; where there is action, there must inevitably be death,—he is always drowned therein, just because he is afraid.

24. 'Some undergo misery for the sake of this world, others meet toil for the sake of heaven; all living beings, wretched through hope and always missing their aim, fall certainly for the sake of happiness into misery.

25. 'It is not the effort itself which I blame,—which flinging aside the base pursues a high path of its own; but the wise, by all this common toil, ought to attain that state in which nothing needs ever to be done again.

26. 'If the mortification of the body here is religion, then the body's happiness is only irreligion; but by religion a man obtains happiness in the next world, therefore religion here bears irreligion as its fruit.

27. 'Since it is only by the mind's authority that the body either acts or ceases to act, therefore to control the thought is alone befitting,—without the thought the body is like a log.

---

[1] Their desired heaven will only be a fresh penance-grove.

28. 'If merit is gained by purity of food, then there is merit also in the deer; and in those men also who live as outcasts from all enjoyments, through being estranged from them by the fault of their destiny.

29. 'If the deliberate choice of pain is a cause of merit, why should not that same choice be directed to pleasure? If you say that the choice of pleasure carries no authority, is not the choice of pain equally without authority?

30. 'So too those who for the sake of purifying their actions, earnestly sprinkle water on themselves, saying, "this is a sacred spot,"—even there this satisfaction resides only in the heart,—for waters will not cleanse away sin.

31. 'The water which has been touched by the virtuous,—that is the spot, if you wish for a sacred spot on the earth; therefore I count as a place of pilgrimage only the virtues of a virtuous man[1],—water without doubt is only water.'

32. Thus he uttered his discourse full of various arguments, and the sun went down into the west; then he entered the grove where penances had now ceased and whose trees were gray with the smoke of the (evening) oblations;

33. Where the sacred fires had been duly transferred when kindled to other spots,—all crowded with the holy hermits who had performed their ablutions, and with the shrines of the gods murmuring with the muttered prayers,—it seemed all alive like the full service of religion in exercise.

34. He spent several nights there, himself like

---

[1] Guṅân eva?

the moon, examining their penances; and he departed from that penance-field, feeling that he had comprehended the whole nature of penance.

35. The dwellers of the hermitage followed him with their minds fixed on the greatness of soul visible in his person, as if they were great seers beholding Religion herself, withdrawn from a land invaded by the base.

36. Then he looked on all those ascetics with their matted hair, bark garments, and rag-strips waving, and he stood considering their penances under an auspicious and noble tree by the way-side.

37. Then the hermits having approached stood surrounding the best of men; and an old man from among them thus addressed him respectfully in a gentle voice:

38. 'At thy coming the hermitage seems to have become full, it becomes as it were empty when thou art gone,—therefore, my son, thou wilt not surely desert it, as the loved life the body of one who wishes to live.

39. 'In front stands the holy mountain Himavat, inhabited by Brahmarshis, râgarshis, and surarshis; by whose mere presence the merit of these penances becomes multiplied to the ascetics.

40. 'Near us also are holy spots of pilgrimage, which become ladders to heaven; loved by divine sages and saints whose souls are intent on devotion and who keep their souls in perfect control.

41. 'From hence, again, the Northern quarter is especially to be fitly followed for the sake of pre-eminent merit; even one who was wise starting towards the south could not advance one single step.

42. 'Hast thou seen in this sacred grove one who

neglects all ceremonies or who follows confused ceremonies or an outcast or one impure, that thou dost not desire to dwell here? Speak it out, and let the abode be welcomed.

43. 'These hermits here desire thee as their companion in penance, thee who art like a storehouse of penance,—to dwell with thee who art like Indra would bring prosperity even to V*ri*haspati.'

44. He, the chief of the wise, when thus addressed in the midst of the ascetics by their chief—having resolved in his mind to put an end to all existence—thus uttered his inward thought:

45. 'The upright-souled saints, the upholders of religion, become the very ideal of our own kindred through their delight in showing hospitality; by all these kind feelings of thine towards me affection is produced in me and the path which regards the self as supreme[1] is revealed.

46. 'I seem to be all at once bathed by these gentle heart-touching words of thine, and the joy now throbs in me once more which I felt when I first grasped the idea of dharma.

47. 'There is sorrow to me when I reflect that I shall have to depart, leaving you who are thus engaged, you who are such a refuge and who have shown such excessive kindness to me,—just as there was when I had to leave my kindred behind.

48. 'But this devotion of yours is for the sake of heaven,—while my desire is that there may be no fresh birth; therefore I wish not to dwell in this wood; the nature of cessation is different from that of activity.

49. 'It is not therefore any dislike on my part or

---

[1] Obscure, cf. Mahâbh. V, 1593.

the wrong conduct of another, which makes me go away from this wood; for ye are all like great sages, standing fast in the religious duties which are in accordance with former ages.'

50. Then having heard the prince's discourse, gracious and of deep meaning, gentle, strong, and full of dignity, the ascetics paid him especial honour.

51. But a certain Brâhman who was lying there in the ashes, tall and wearing his hair in a tuft, and clothed in the bark of trees, with reddish eyes and a thin long nose, and carrying a pot with water[1] in his hand, thus lifted his voice:

52. 'O sage, brave indeed is thy purpose, who, young as thou art, hast seen the evils of birth; he who, having pondered thoroughly heaven and liberation, makes up his mind for liberation,—he is indeed brave!

53. 'By all those various sacrifices, penances, and vows the slaves of passion desire to go to heaven; but the strong, having battled with passion as with an enemy, desire to obtain liberation.

54. 'If this is thy settled purpose, go quickly to Vindhyakosh*th*a; the Muni Arâ*d*a lives there who has gained an insight into absolute bliss.

55. 'From him thou wilt hear the path to truth, and if thou hast a desire for it, thou wilt embrace it; but as I foresee, this purpose of thine will go on further, after having rejected his theory.

56. 'With the nose of a well-fed horse, large long eyes, a red lower lip, white sharp teeth, and a thin red tongue,—this face of thine will drink up the entire ocean of what is to be known.

---

[1] Conjectural. Dr. von Böhtlingk suggests ku*md*âvahasto, 'the back of whose hand was like a ku*md*a.'

57. 'That unfathomed depth which characterises thee, that majesty and all those signs of thine,—they shall win a teacher's chair in the earth which was never won by sages even in a former age.'

58. The prince replied, 'Very well,' and having saluted the company of sages he departed; the hermits also having duly performed to him all the rites of courtesy entered again into the ascetic-grove.

BOOK VIII.

1. Meanwhile the attendant of the horse, in deep distress, when his unselfish master thus went into the forest, made every effort in the road to dissolve[1] his load of sorrow, and yet in spite of it all not a tear dropped from him.

2. But the road which by his lord's command he had traversed in one night with that horse,—that same road he now travelled in eight days, pondering his lord's absence.

3. And the horse Ka*m*thaka, though he still went on bravely, flagged and had lost all spirit in his heart; and decked though he was with ornaments, he had lost all his beauty when bereft of his master.

4. And turning round towards that ascetic-grove, he neighed repeatedly with a mournful sound; and though pressed with hunger, he welcomed not nor tasted any grass or water on the road, as before[2].

5. Slowly they two at last came back to the city called after Kapila, which seemed empty when deserted by that hero who was bent on the

---

[1] Vigraha seems here used in an unusual sense. Cf. Tennyson's 'Home they brought her warrior dead, &c.'

[2] I read nâbhinananda, supposing na to have been written on the margin and inserted in the wrong place, otherwise abhis must be used for abhi. [This is confirmed by the Tibetan, which translates abhinananda by mṅon-par ma dga, where mṅon-par is the usual translation of the preposition abhi. H.W.]

salvation of the world,—like the sky bereft of the sun.

6. Bright as it was with lotus-covered waters, adorned also with trees full of flowers, that garden of his, which was now like a forest, was no longer gay with citizens who had lost all their gladness.

7. Then those two,—who were as it were silently forbidden by the sad inhabitants who were wandering in that direction, their brightness gone and their eyes dim with tears,—slowly entered the city which seemed all bathed in gloom.

8. Having heard that they had returned with their limbs all relaxed, coming back without the pride of the *S*âkya race, the men of the city shed tears in the road, as when in old days the chariot of the son of Da*s*aratha came back.

9. Full of wrath, the people followed *Kha*m*daka in the road, crying behind him with tears, 'Where is the king's son, the glory of his race and kingdom? he has been stolen away by thee.'

10. Then he said to those faithful ones, 'I have not left the king's son; but by him in the uninhabited forest I weeping and the dress of a householder were abandoned together.'

11. Having heard these words of his those crowds adopted a most difficult resolve; they did not wipe away the tears which fell from their eyes, and they blamed their own (evil) hearts on account of the consequences of their actions;

12. Then they said, 'Let us go this very day into that forest, whither he is gone, whose gait is like the king of elephants; without him we have no wish to live, like the senses when the souls depart.

13. 'This city bereft of him is a forest, and that forest which possesses him is a city; the city without him has no charms for us, like heaven without the lord of the Maruts, when V*ri*tra was slain[1].'

14. Next the women crowded to the rows of windows, crying to one another, 'The prince has returned;' but having heard that his horse had an empty back, they closed the windows again and wailed aloud.

15. But the king, having undertaken religious observances for the recovery of his son, with his mind distressed by the vow and the sorrow, was muttering prayers in the temple, and performing such rites as suited the occasion.

16. Then with his eyes filled with tears,—taking the horse, his whole soul fixed on the horse,—overcome with grief he[2] entered the palace as if his master had been killed by an enemy.

17. And entering the royal stable, looking about with his eyes full of tears, Ka*m*thaka uttered a loud sound, as if he were uttering his woe to the people.

18. Then the birds that fed in the middle of the house, and the carefully cherished horses that were tied near by, re-echoed the sound of that horse, thinking that it might be the return of the prince.

19. And the people, deceived by an excessive joy, who were in the neighbourhood of the king's inner apartments, thought in their hearts, 'Since the horse Ka*m*thaka neighs, it must be that the prince is coming.'

20. Then the women, who were fainting with

---

[1] Quoted by U*gg*valadatta, on U*n*âdi-sûtras I, 156.
[2] Sc. *Kh*andaka.

sorrow, now in wild joy, with their eyes rolling to see the prince, rushed out of the palace full of hope, like flickering lightnings from an autumn cloud.

21. With their dress hanging down, and their linen garments soiled, their faces untouched by collyrium and with eyes dimmed by tears; dark and discoloured and destitute of all painting[1], like the stars in the sky, pale-red with the ending of night;

22. With their feet unstained by red, and undecked by anklets,—their faces without earrings, and their ears in their native simplicity,—their loins with only nature's fulness, and uncircled by any girdle,—and their bosoms bare of strings of pearls as if they had been robbed.

23. But when they saw *Kh*andaka standing helpless, his eyes filled with tears, and the horse, the noble women wept with pale faces, like cows abandoned by the bull in the midst of the forest.

24. Then the king's principal queen Gautamî, like a fond cow that has lost her calf, fell bursting into tears on the ground with outstretched arms, like a golden plantain-tree with trembling leaves.

25. Some of the other women, bereft of their brightness and with arms and souls lifeless, and seeming to have lost their senses in their despondency, raised no cry, shed no tear, and breathed not, standing senseless as if painted[2].

26. Others as having lost all self-control, fainting in their sorrow for their lord, their faces pouring tears from their eyes, watered their bosoms from

---

[1] Is a*ñg*ana*y*â used here irregularly in the fem. to distinguish it from a*ñg*ana, ' the pinguent?'

[2] Conjectural.

which all sandal-wood was banished, like a mountain the rocks with its streams.

27. Then that royal palace was illumined with their faces pelted by the tears from their eyes, as a lake in the time of the first rains with its dripping lotuses pelted by the rain from the clouds.

28. The noble women beat their breasts with their lotus-like hands, falling incessantly, whose fingers were round and plump, which had their arteries hidden and bore no ornaments,—as creepers tossed by the wind strike themselves with their shoots.

29. And again how those women shone forth, as their bosoms rose up together after the blow from the hand, and trembled with the shock,—like the streams, when their pairs of ruddy geese shake, as the lotuses on which they sit wave about with the wind from the wood [1].

30. As they pressed their breasts with their hands, so too they pressed their hands with their breasts,—dull to all feelings of pity, they made their hands and bosoms inflict mutual pains on each other.

31. Then thus spoke Ya*s*odharâ, shedding tears with deep [2] sorrow, her bosom heaving with her sighs, her eyes discoloured with anger, and her voice choking with emotion through the influence of despondency:

32. 'Leaving me helplessly asleep in the night, whither, O *Kha*ṃdaka, is he, the desire of my heart,

---

[1] This is an obscure verse,—yathâpi is not clear; I have taken yathâ as a 'how' of admiration. The latter lines seem to compare the hand swaying with the motion of the bosom to the bird seated on the tossed lotus.

[2] Is vigâdha for agâdha, or should we read vigâ*dh*a?

gone? and when thou and Ka*m*thaka are alone come back, while three went away together, my mind trembles.

33. 'Why dost thou weep to-day, O cruel one, having done a dishonourable, pitiless, and unfriendly deed to me? Cease thy tears and be content in thy heart,—tears and that deed of thine ill agree.

34. 'Through thee, his dear obedient faithful loyal companion, always doing what was right, the son of my lord is gone never to return,—rejoice,—all hail! thy pains have gained their end.

35. 'Better for a man a wise enemy rather than a foolish friend unskilled in emergencies; by thee, the unwise self-styled friend, a great calamity has been brought upon this family.

36. 'These women are sorely to be pitied who have put away their ornaments, having their eyes red and dimmed with continuous tears, who are as it were desolate widows, though their lord still stands as unshaken as the earth or Mount Himavat.

37. 'And these lines of palaces seem to weep aloud, flinging up their dovecots for arms, with the long unbroken moan of their doves,—separated verily, with him, from all who could restrain them.

38. 'Even that horse Ka*m*thaka without doubt desired my utter ruin; for he bore away from hence my treasure when all were sound asleep in the night,—like one who steals jewels.

39. 'When he was able to bear even the onsets of arrows, and still more the strokes of whips,—how then for fear of the fall of a whip, could he go carrying with him my prosperity and my heart together?

40. 'The base creature now neighs loudly, filling the king's palace with the sound; but when he

carried away my beloved, then this vilest of horses was dumb.

41. 'If he had neighed and so woke up the people, or had even made a noise with his hoofs on the ground, or had made the loudest sound he could with his jaws, my grief would not have been so great.'

42. Having thus heard the queen's words, their syllables choked with tears and full of lament, slowly *Kha*mdaka uttered this answer, with his face bent down, his voice low with tears, and his hands clasped in supplication:

43. 'Surely, O queen, thou wilt not blame Ka*m*thaka nor wilt thou show thy anger against me,—know that we two are entirely guiltless,—that god amongst men, O queen, is gone away like a god.

44. 'I indeed, though I well knew the king's command, as though dragged by force by some divine powers, brought quickly to him this swift steed, and followed him on the road unwearied.

45. 'And this best of horses as he went along touched not the ground with the tips of his hoofs as if they were kept aloft from it; and so too, having his mouth restrained as by fate, he made no sound with his jaws and neighed not.

46. 'When the prince went out, then the gate was thrown open of its own accord; and the darkness of the night was, as it were, pierced by the sun,—we may learn from hence too that this was the ordering of fate.

47. 'When also by the king's command, in palace and city, diligent guards had been placed by thousands, and at that time they were all overcome by sleep and woke not,—we may learn from hence too that this was the ordering of fate.

48. 'When also the garment, approved for a

hermit's dwelling in the forest, was offered to him at the moment by some denizen of heaven, and the tiara which he threw into the sky was carried off, —we may learn from hence too that this was the ordering of fate.

49. 'Do not therefore assume[1] that his departure arises from the fault of either of us, O queen; neither I nor this horse acted by our own choice; he went on his way with the gods as his retinue.'

50. Having thus heard the history of the prince's departure, so marvellous in many ways, those women, as though losing their grief, were filled with wonder, but they again took up their distress at the thought of his becoming an ascetic.

51. With her eyes filled with the tears of despondency, wretched like an osprey who has lost her young,—Gautamî abandoning all self-control wailed aloud,—she fainted, and with a weeping face exclaimed:

52. 'Beautiful, soft, black, and all in great waves, growing each from its own special root,—those hairs of his are tossed on the ground, worthy to be encircled by a royal diadem.

53. 'With his long arms and lion-gait, his bull-like eye, and his beauty bright like gold, his broad chest, and his voice deep as a drum or a cloud,—should such a hero as this dwell in a hermitage?

54. 'This earth is indeed unworthy as regards that peerless doer of noble actions, for such a virtuous hero has gone away from her,—it is the merits and virtues of the subjects which produce their king.

55. 'Those two feet of his, tender, with their

---

[1] Should we read pratipattum for pratigantum?

beautiful web spread between the toes, with their ankles concealed, and soft like a blue lotus,—how can they, bearing a wheel marked in the middle, walk on the hard ground of the skirts of the forest?

56. 'That body, which deserves to sit or lie on the roof of a palace,— honoured with costly garments, aloes, and sandal-wood,—how will that manly body live in the woods, exposed to the attacks of the cold, the heat, and the rain?

57. 'He who was proud of his family, goodness, strength, energy, sacred learning, beauty, and youth, —who was ever ready to give, not to ask,—how will he go about begging alms from others?

58. 'He who, lying on a spotless golden bed, was awakened during the night by the concert of musical instruments,—how alas! will he, my ascetic, sleep to-day on the bare ground with only one rag of cloth interposed?'

59. Having heard this piteous lamentation, the women, embracing one another with their arms, rained the tears from their eyes, as the shaken creepers drop honey from their flowers.

60. Then Yasodharâ fell upon the ground, like the ruddy goose parted from her mate, and in utter bewilderment she slowly lamented, with her voice repeatedly stopped by sobs:

61. 'If he wishes to practise a religious life after abandoning me his lawful wife widowed,—where is his religion, who wishes to follow penance without his lawful wife to share it with him?

62. 'He surely has never heard of the monarchs of olden times, his own ancestors, Mahâsudarsa[1] and

---

[1] Mahâsudassana is the name of a king in *G*âtaka I, 95.

the rest,—how they went with their wives into the forest,—that he thus wishes to follow a religious life without me.

63. 'He does not see that husband and wife are both consecrated in sacrifices, and both purified by the performance of the rites of the Veda, and both destined to enjoy[1] the same results afterwards,—he therefore grudges me a share in his merit.

64. 'Surely it must be that this fond lover of religion, knowing that my mind was secretly quarrelling even with my beloved, lightly and without fear has deserted me thus angry, in the hope to obtain heavenly nymphs in Indra's world!

65. 'But what kind of a thought is this of mine? those women even there have the attributes which belong to bodies,—for whose sake he thus practises austerities in the forest, deserting his royal magnificence and my fond devotion.

66. 'I have no such longing for the joy of heaven, nor is that hard for even common people to win if they are resolute[2]; but my one desire is how he my beloved may never leave me either in this world or the next.

67. 'Even if I am unworthy to look on my husband's face with its long eyes and bright smile, still is this poor Râhula never to roll about in his father's lap?

68. 'Alas! the mind of that wise hero is terribly stern,—gentle as his beauty seems, it is pitilessly cruel,—who can desert of his own accord such an infant son with his inarticulate talk, one who would charm even an enemy.

69. 'My heart too is certainly most stern, yea,

---

[1] I read bubhukshû for bubhukshuḥ.
[2] Api, I think, should properly follow ganasya.

made of rock or fashioned even of iron, which does not break when its lord is gone to the forest, deserted by his royal glory like an orphan,—he so well worthy of happiness.'

70. So the queen, fainting in her woe, wept and pondered and wailed aloud repeatedly,—self-possessed as she was by nature, yet in her distress she remembered not her fortitude and felt no shame.

71. Seeing Yasodharâ thus bewildered with her wild utterances of grief and fallen on the ground, all the women cried out with their faces streaming with tears like large lotuses beaten by the rain.

72. But the king, having ended his prayers, and performed the auspicious rites of the sacrifice, now came out of the temple; and being smitten by the wailing sound of the people, he tottered like an elephant at the crash of a thunderbolt.

73. Having heard (of the arrival) of both *Kham*daka and Ka*m*thaka, and having learned the fixed resolve of his son, the lord of the earth fell struck down by sorrow like the banner of Indra when the festival is over [1].

74. Then the king, distracted by his grief for his son, being held up for a moment by his attendants all of the same race, gazed on the horse with his eyes filled with tears, and then falling on the ground wailed aloud:

75. 'After having done many dear exploits for me in battle, one great deed of cruelty, O Ka*m*thaka, hast thou done,—for by thee that dear son of mine, dear for his every virtue, has been tossed down in the wood, dear as he was, like a worthless thing.

---

[1] Cf. I, 63.

76. 'Therefore either lead me to-day where he is, or go quickly and bring him back again; without him there is no life left to me, as to one plunged in sickness without the true medicine.

77. 'When Suvar*n*anish*th*ivin was carried away by death, it seemed impossible that S*ri*mgaya¹ should not die; and shall I, when my duty-loving son is gone, fear to set my soul free, like any coward?

78. 'How should not the mind of Manu himself be distracted, when parted from his dear virtuous son², —(Manu) the son of Vivasvat, who knew the higher and the lower, the mighty lord of creatures, the institutor of the ten chieftains³.

79. 'I envy the monarch, that friend of Indra, the wise son of king A*g*a⁴, who, when his son went into the forest, went himself to heaven, and dragged out no miserable life here with vain tears.

80. 'Describe to me, O beloved one, the court of that hermitage, whither thou hast carried him who is as my funeral oblation of water; these my vital airs are all ready to depart, and are eager for it, longing to drink it.'

81. Thus the king, in his grief for his separation from his son,—losing all his innate firmness which was stedfast like the earth,—loudly lamented as one distraught, like Da*s*aratha, a prey to his sorrow for Râma.

---

¹ See Mahâbh. XII, 31. The MSS. read Sa*m*gaya for S*ri*mgaya.
² Does this refer to his losing his son Sudyumna, who was changed to a woman, Vish*n*u Pur. IV, 1?
³ Da*s*akshatrak*ri*t is an obscure phrase; [the Tibetan renders it by rgyal-rigs bcu byas, 'king-race ten made;' rgyal-rigs is the ordinary translation of kshatriya. H.W.]
⁴ Da*s*aratha.

82. Then the wise counsellor, endued with religious learning, courtesy, and virtue, and the old family priest, spoke to him as was befitting in these well-weighed words, neither with their faces overwhelmed by grief nor yet wholly unmoved:

83. 'Cease, O noblest of men, thy grief, regain thy firmness,—surely thou wilt not, O firm hero, shed tears like one of no self-control; many kings on this earth have gone into the forests, throwing away their royal pomp like a crushed wreath.

84. 'Moreover, this his state of mind was all pre-determined; remember those words long ago of the holy sage Asita; "He will never be made to dwell even for a moment contentedly in heaven or in an emperor's domain."

85. 'But if, O best of men, the effort must be made, quickly speak the word, we two will at once go together; let the battle be waged in every way with thy son and his fate whatever it be.'

86. Then the king commanded them both, 'Do you both go quickly hence,—my heart will not return to quiet, any more than a bird's in the woods longing for its young.'

87. With a prompt acquiescence at the king's order the counsellor and the family priest went to that forest; and then with his wives and his queen the king also, saying, 'It is done,' performed the remainder of the rites.

BOOK IX.

1. Then the two, the counsellor and the family priest, beaten by the king with his scourge of tears, went with every effort to that forest in the hurry of affection, like two noble horses goaded.

2. Having come at last full of weariness to that hermitage, accompanied by a fitting train,—they dismissed their royal pomp and with sober gestures entered the abode of Bhârgava.

3. Having saluted that Brâhman with due respect, and having been honoured by him with due reverence in return, having seated themselves, plunging at once into the subject, they addressed Bhârgava, who was likewise seated, concerning their errand.

4. 'Let your honour know us to be respectively imperfect proficients in preserving the sacred learning and in retaining the state-counsels,—in the service of the monarch of the Ikshvâku race, pure in his valour and pure and wide in his glory.

5. 'His son, who is like Gayanta, while he himself is like Indra, has come here, it is said, desirous to escape from the fear of old age and death,—know that we two are come here on account of him.'

6. He answered them, 'That prince of the long arms did indeed come here, but not as one unawakened; "this dharma only brings us back again," —recognising this, he went off forthwith towards Arâda, seeking liberation.'

7. Then they two, having understood the true

state of things, bade that Brâhman at once farewell, and wearied though they were, went on as if they were unwearied, thither whither the prince was gone.

8. As they were going, they saw him bereft of all ornaments[1], but still radiant with his beauty, sitting like a king in the road at the foot of a tree, like the sun under the canopy of a cloud.

9. Leaving his chariot, the family priest then went up to the prince with the counsellor, as the saint Aurva*s*eya[2] went with Vâmadeva, wishing to see Râma when he dwelt in the forest.

10. They paid him honour as was fitting, as *S*ukra and A*m*giras honoured Indra in heaven; and he in return paid due honour to them, as Indra in heaven to *S*ukra and A*m*giras.

11. Then they, having obtained his permission, sat down near him who was the banner of the *S*âkya race; and they shone in his proximity like the two stars of the asterism Punarvasû in conjunction with the moon.

12. The family priest addressed the prince who shone brightly as he sat at the foot of the tree, as V*ri*haspati addressed Indra's son *G*ayanta, seated in heaven under the heavenly tree pâri*g*âta:

13. 'O prince, consider for a moment what the king with his eyes raining tears said to thee, as he lay fainting on the ground with the arrow of thy sorrow plunged into his heart.

14. '"I know that thy resolve is fixed upon religion, and I am convinced that this purpose of thine is unchanging[3]; but I am consumed with a flame of

---

[1] Is s*rig*ayâ for s*r*a*g*â?

[2] Agastya, the son of Urva*s*î. Vâmadeva was Da*s*aratha's counsellor.

[3] Conjectural. [The Tibetan reads the second line, khyod-kyi

anguish like fire at thy flying to the woods at an inopportune time.

15. '"Come, thou who lovest duty, for the sake of what is my heart's desire,—abandon this purpose for the sake of duty; this huge swollen stream of sorrow sweeps me away as a river's torrent its bank.

16. '"That effect' which is wrought in the clouds, water, the dry grass, and the mountains by the wind, the sun, the fire, and the thunderbolt,—that same effect this grief produces in us by its tearing in pieces, its drying up, its burning, and its cleaving.

17. '"Enjoy therefore for a while the sovereignty of the earth,—thou shalt go to the forest at the time provided by the *sástras*,—do not show disregard for thy unhappy kindred,—compassion for all creatures is the true religion.

18. '"Religion is not wrought out only in the forests, the salvation of ascetics can be accomplished even in a city; thought and effort are the true means; the forest and the badge are only a coward's signs.

19. '"Liberation has been attained even by householders, Indras among men, who wore diadems, and carried strings of pearls suspended on their shoulders, whose garlands were entangled with bracelets, and who lay cradled in the lap of Fortune.

20. '"Bali and Vagrabâhu, the two younger brothers of Dhruva, Vaibhrâga, Âshâ*dh*a, and A*n*ti-

---

byuṅ-var ,gyur-var don-ni ç̇es-pao, 'I know thy purpose which is about to arise (or which has arisen) in thy mind.' Can they have read bhâvinam or bhâvitam? H.W.]

¹ I read v*r*itti*h*.

deva¹, and *G*anaka also, the king of the Videhas, and king Sena*g*it's son, his tree of ripe blessing²;

21. '"Know that all these great kings who were householders were well skilled in attaining the merit which leads to final bliss,—do thou also therefore obtain both³ simultaneously—royal magnificence and the control over the mind.

22. '"I desire,—when I have once closely embraced thee after thy kingly consecration is once performed, and while thou art still wet with the sacred water,—when I behold thee with the pomp of the royal umbrella,—in the fulness of that joy to enter the forest."

23. 'Thus did the king say to thee in a speech whose words were stopped by tears,—surely having heard it, for the sake of what is so dear to him, thou wilt with all affection follow his affection.

24. 'The king of the *S*âkyas is drowned in a deep sea of sorrow, full of waves of trouble, springing from thee; do thou therefore deliver him helpless and protectorless like an ox drowning in the sea.

25. 'Having heard that Bhîshma who sprang from Gangâ's womb, Râma, and Râma the son of Bh*r*igu, —all did what would please their fathers;—surely thou too wilt do thy father's desire.

26. 'Consider also the queen, who brought thee

---

¹ Cf. I, 57; IX, 60.

² My reading pâkadrumam is conjectural, Pâradrumau as two old kings would be a possible reading. Sena*g*it's son is praised for his philosophical depth in Mahâbh. XII, 6524, &c.; he is there called Medhâvin. [The Tibetan has brtan-pai (dhruva) nu vo, 'the firm one's younger brother (?);' it also has ₀gro dań ljon-çin-can for pâkadruma, 'having a tree of—?' It takes senagita*sk*a râg*ñ*a*h* as acc. plural. II. W.]

³ Ubhe⁕pi, although with pragr*i*hya e.

up, who has not yet gone to the region inhabited by Agastya[1]—wilt thou not take some heed of her, who ceaselessly grieves like a fond cow that has lost her calf?

27. 'Surely thou wilt succour thy wife by the sight of thee, who now mourns widowed yet with her lord still alive,—like a swan separated from her mate or a female elephant deserted in the forest by her companion.

28. 'Thy only son, a child little deserving such woe, distressed with sorrow, and[2] . . . . —O deliver Râhula from the grief of his kindred like the full moon from the contact of Râhu!

29. 'Burned with the fire of anguish within him, to which thy absence adds fresh fuel,—a fire whose smoke is sighs and its flame despair,—he wanders for a sight of thee through the women's apartments and the whole city.'

30. The Bodhisattva,—whose perfection was absolute,—having heard the words of the family priest, reflected for a moment, knowing all the virtues of the virtuous, and then thus uttered his gentle reply:

31. 'I well know the paternal tenderness[3] of the king, especially that which he has displayed towards me; yet knowing this as I do, still alarmed at sickness, old age, and death, I am inevitably forced to leave my kindred.

32. 'Who would not wish to see his dear kindred, if but this separation from beloved ones did not exist? but since even after it has been once, separa-

---

[1] The south,—the region of the god of death.
[2] Five syllables are here lost,—apakvasattvam?
[3] Should we read tanayaprasaktam?

tion will still come again, it is for this that I abandon my father, however loving.

33. 'I do not however approve that thou shouldst consider the king's grief as caused by me, when in the midst of his dream-like unions he is afflicted by thoughts of separations in the future.

34. 'Thus let thy thoughts settle into certainty, having seen the multiform in its various developments; neither a son nor kindred is the cause of sorrow,—this sorrow is only caused by ignorance.

35. 'Since parting is inevitably fixed in the course of time for all beings, just as for travellers who have joined company on a road,—what wise man would cherish sorrow, when he loses his kindred, even though he loves them [1]?

36. 'Leaving his kindred in another world, he departs hither; and having stolen away [2] from them here, he goes forth once more; " having gone thither, go thou elsewhere also,"—such is the lot of mankind,—what consideration can the yogin have for them [3]?

37. 'Since from the moment of leaving the womb death is a characteristic adjunct [4], why, in thy affection for thy son, hast thou called my departure to the forest ill-timed?

38. 'There may be an "ill time" in one's attaining a worldly object,—time indeed is described as

---

[1] Some letters are here lost in the original.

[2] Pralabhya, cf. Horace, 'vivens moriensque fefellit.' [The Tibetan has rab-tu bslas-nas, 'having deceived.' H.W.]

[3] The Tibetan has for the fourth line de-ltar (evam) ,dor-ldan skye-la rjes-su rten rnam ci, 'thus what kind of reliance is there on man who is of a leaving disposition?' Should we read in the original ityevam gane tyâgini ko*nurodhah?

[4] Can anubadhâya be wrongly used for anubandhâya?

inseparably connected with all things[1]; time drags the world into all its various times; but all time suits a bliss which is really worthy of praise[2].

39. 'That the king should wish to surrender to me his kingdom,—this is a noble thought, well worthy of a father; but it would be as improper for me to accept it, as for a sick man through greed to accept unwholesome food.

40. 'How can it be right for the wise man to enter royalty, the home of illusion, where are found anxiety, passion, and weariness, and the violation of all right through another's service?

41. 'The golden palace seems to me to be on fire; the daintiest viands seem mixed with poison; infested with crocodiles[3] [is the tranquil lotus-bed].'

. . . .

42. Having heard the king's son uttering this discourse, well suitable to his virtues and knowledge of the soul, freed from all desires, full of sound reasons, and weighty,—the counsellor thus made answer:

43. 'This resolve of thine is an excellent counsel, not unfit in itself but only unfit at the present time; it could not be thy duty, loving duty as thou dost, to leave thy father in his old age to sorrow.

44. 'Surely thy mind is not very penetrating, or it is ill-skilled in examining duty, wealth, and pleasure[4],—when for the sake of an unseen result thou departest disregarding a visible end.

---

[1] Cf. Pân. III, 3, 44.
[2] I.e. mukti can never be ill-timed. But this is an obscure *sloka*.
[3] The remainder of the prince's speech is lost. By Beal's translation from the Chinese, fifteen verses are wanting.
[4] The three well-known 'secular' ends of human action.

45. 'Again, some say that there is another birth,—others with confident assertion say that there is not; since then the matter is all in doubt, it is right to enjoy the good fortune which comes into thy hand.

46. 'If there is any activity hereafter, we will enjoy ourselves in it as may offer; or if there is no activity beyond this life, then there is an assured liberation to all the world without any effort.

47. 'Some say there is a future life, but they do not allow the possibility of liberation; as fire is hot by nature and water liquid, so they hold that there is a special nature in our power of action[1].

48. 'Some maintain that all things arise from inherent properties,—both good and evil and existence and non-existence; and since all this world thus arises spontaneously, therefore also all effort of ours is vain.

49. 'Since the action of the senses is fixed, and so too the agreeableness or the disagreeableness of outward objects,—then for that which is united to old age and pains, what effort can avail to alter it? Does it not all arise spontaneously?

50. 'The fire becomes quenched by water, and fire causes[2] water to evaporate; and different elements, united in a body, producing unity, bear up the world.

51. 'That the nature of the embryo in the womb is produced as composed of hands, feet, belly, back, and head, and that it is also united with the soul,—the wise declare that all this comes of itself spontaneously.

52. 'Who causes the sharpness of the thorn? or

---

[1] I.e. it cannot be abolished.   [2] I read gamayanti.

the various natures of beasts and birds? All this has arisen spontaneously; there is no acting from desire, how then can there be such a thing as will?

53. 'Others say that creation comes from Îsvara,— what need then is there of the effort of the conscious soul¹? That which is the cause of the action of the world, is also determined as the cause of its ceasing to act.

54. 'Some say that the coming into being and the destruction of being are alike caused by the soul; but they say that coming into being arises without effort, while the attainment of liberation is by effort.

55. 'A man discharges his debt to his ancestors by begetting offspring, to the saints by sacred lore, to the gods by sacrifices; he is born with these three debts upon him, — whoever has liberation (from these,) he indeed has liberation.

56. 'Thus by this series of rules the wise promise liberation to him who uses effort; but however ready for effort with all their energy, those who seek liberation will find weariness.

57. 'Therefore, gentle youth, if thou hast a love for liberation, follow rightly the prescribed rule; thus wilt thou thyself attain to it, and the king's grief will come to an end.

58. 'And as for thy meditations on the evils of life ending in thy return from the forest to thy home,—let not the thought of this trouble thee, my son,—those in old time also have returned from the forests to their houses.

59. 'The king A*m*barisha², though he had

---

¹ Purusha.   ² Probably the son of Nâbhâga.

dwelt in the forest, went back to the city, surrounded by his children; so too Râma, seeing the earth oppressed by the base, came forth from his hermitage and ruled it again.

60. 'So too Drumâksha, the king of the *S*âlvas, came to his city from the forest with his son; and Sâ*m*kr*i*ti A*m*tideva¹, after he had become a Brahmarshi, received his royal dignity from the saint Va*s*ish*th*a.

61. 'Such men as these, illustrious in glory and virtue, left the forests and came back to their houses; therefore it is no sin to return from a hermitage to one's home, if it be only for the sake of duty.'

62. Then having heard the affectionate and loyal words of the minister, who was as the eye of the king,—firm in his resolve, the king's son made his answer, with nothing omitted or displaced², neither tedious³ nor hasty:

63. 'This doubt whether anything exists or not, is not to be solved for me by another's words; having determined the truth by asceticism or quietism, I will myself grasp whatever is ascertained concerning it.

64. 'It is not for me to accept a theory which depends on the unknown and is all controverted, and which involves a hundred prepossessions; what

---

¹ This might mean A*m*tideva (cf. I, 57, IX, 20) the son of Sa*m*kr*i*ti, but in Mahâbh. XII,1013 we have Ra*m*tideva the son of Sa*m*kr*i*ti; cf. Burnouf on Rudraka and Udraka, Introduction, p. 386. [The Tibetan takes sâ*m*kr*i*ti as sbyin-sreg-da*n*-bcas, 'together with burnt offering.' H.W.] Would this imply an old reading sâhuti?—For A*m*tideva's connection with Va*s*ish*th*a see Mahâbh. XII, 8591.

² I read avyastam.
³ Or 'prejudiced?'

wise man would go by another's belief? Mankind are like the blind directed in the darkness by the blind.

65. 'But even though I cannot discern the truth, yet still, if good and evil are doubted, let one's mind be set on the good; even a toil[1] in vain is to be chosen by him whose soul is good, while the man of base soul has no joy even in the truth.

66. 'But having seen that this "sacred tradition" is uncertain, know that that only is right which has been uttered by the trustworthy; and know that trustworthiness means the absence of faults; he who is without faults will not utter an untruth.

67. 'And as for what thou saidst to me in regard to my returning to my home, by alleging Râma and others as examples, they are no authority,—for in determining duty, how canst thou quote as authorities those who have broken their vows?

68. 'Even the sun, therefore, may fall to the earth, even the mountain Himavat may lose its firmness; but never would I return to my home as a man of the world, with no knowledge of the truth and my senses only alert for external objects.

69. 'I would enter the blazing fire, but not my house with my purpose unfulfilled.' Thus he proudly made his resolve, and rising up in accordance with it, full of disinterestedness, went his way.

70. Then the minister and the Brâhman, both full of tears, having heard his firm determination, and having followed him awhile with despondent

---

[1] MSS. khedo.

looks, and overcome with sorrow, slowly returned of necessity to the city.

71. Through their love for the prince and their devotion to the king, they returned, and often stopped looking back[1]; they could neither behold him on the road nor yet lose the sight of him,— shining in his own splendour and beyond the reach of all others, like the sun.

72. Having placed faithful emissaries in disguise to find out the actions of him who was the supreme refuge of all, they went on with faltering steps, saying to each other, 'How shall we approach the king and see him, who is longing for his dear son?'

---

[1] Another reading gives 'full of reproach.'

BOOK X.

1. The prince, he of the broad and lusty chest, having thus dismissed the minister and the priest, crossed the Ganges with its speeding waves and went to Râgagriha with its beautiful palaces.

2. He reached the city distinguished by the five hills, well guarded and adorned with mountains, and supported and hallowed by auspicious sacred places[1],—like Brahman[2] in a holy calm going to the uppermost heaven.

3. Having heard of his majesty and strength, and his splendid beauty, surpassing all other men, the people of that region were all astonished as at him who has a bull for his sign and is immovable in his vow[3].

4. On seeing him, he who was going elsewhere stood still, and he who was standing there followed him in the way; he who was walking gently and gravely ran quickly, and he who was sitting at once sprang up.

5. Some people reverenced him with their hands, others in worship saluted him with their heads, some addressed him with affectionate words,—not one went on without paying him homage.

6. Those who were wearing gay-coloured dresses were ashamed when they saw him, those who were talking on random subjects fell to silence on the

---

[1] Tapoda is the name of a tîrtha in Magadha.
[2] Svayambhû.
[3] Siva.

road; no one indulged in an improper thought, as at the presence of Religion herself embodied.

7. In the men and the women on the highway, even though they were intent on other business, that conduct alone with the profoundest reverence seemed proper which is enjoined by the rules of royal homage; but his eyes never looked upon them.

8. His brows, his forehead, his mouth, or his eyes,—his body, his hands, his feet, or his gait,—whatever part of him any one beheld, that at once riveted his eyes.

9. Having beheld him with the beautiful circle of hair between his brows[1] and with long eyes, with his radiant body and his hands showing a graceful membrane between the fingers,—so worthy of ruling the earth and yet wearing a mendicant's dress,—the Goddess of Râgagriha was herself perturbed.

10. Then Srenya[2], the lord of the court of the Magadhas, beheld from the outside of his palace the immense concourse of people, and asked the reason of it; and thus did a man recount it to him:

11. 'He who was thus foretold by the Brâhmans, "he will either attain supreme wisdom or the empire of the earth,"—it is he, the son of the king of the Sâkyas, who is the ascetic whom the people are gazing at.'

12. The king, having heard this and perceived its meaning with his mind, thus at once spoke to that man: 'Let it be known whither he is going;' and the man, receiving the command, followed the prince.

---

[1] So the Tibetan. The Sanskrit text seems corrupt here. Cf. I, 65 c.

[2] A name of Bimbisâra, see Burnouf, Introd. p. 165.

13. With unrestless eyes, seeing only a yoke's length before him¹, with his voice hushed, and his walk slow and measured, he, the noblest of mendicants, went begging alms, keeping his limbs and his wandering thoughts under control.

14. Having received such alms as were offered, he retired to a lonely cascade of the mountain; and having eaten it there in the fitting manner, he ascended the mountain Pâm*d*ava².

15. In that wood, thickly filled with lodhra trees, having its thickets resonant with the notes of the peacocks, he the sun of mankind shone, wearing his red dress, like the morning sun above the eastern mountain.

16. That royal attendant, having thus watched him there, related it all to the king Sre*n*ya; and the king, when he heard it, in his deep veneration, started himself to go thither with a modest retinue.

17. He who was like the Pâm*d*avas in heroism, and like a mountain in stature, ascended Pâm*d*ava, that noblest of mountains,—a crown-wearer, of lion-like gait, a lion among men, as a maned lion ascends a mountain.

18. There he beheld the Bodhisattva, resplendent as he sat on his hams, with subdued senses, as if the mountain were moving³, and he himself were a peak thereof,—like the moon rising from the top of a cloud.

19. Him, distinguished by his beauty of form and perfect tranquillity as the very creation of Religion

---

¹ Hardy explains this 'he does not look before him further than the distance of a plough or nine spans' (Manual of Buddhism, p. 371).

² Cf. Lalitavistara.

³ I.e. as if he, not the mountain, were entitled to the name a*k*ala.

herself,—filled with astonishment and affectionate regard the king of men approached, as Indra the self-existent (Brahman).

20. He, the chief of the courteous, having courteously drawn nigh to him, inquired as to the equilibrium of his bodily humours; and the other with equal gentleness assured the king of his health of mind and freedom from all ailments.

21. Then the king sat down on the clean surface of the rock, dark blue like an elephant's ear; and being seated[1], with the other's assent, he thus spoke, desiring to know his state of mind:

22. 'I have a strong friendship with thy family, come down by inheritance and well proved; since from this a desire to speak to thee, my son, has arisen in me, therefore listen to my words of affection.

23. 'When I consider thy widespread race, beginning with the sun, thy fresh youth, and thy conspicuous beauty,—whence comes this resolve of thine so out of all harmony with the rest, set wholly on a mendicant's life, not on a kingdom?

24. 'Thy limbs are worthy of red sandal-wood[2] perfumes,—they do not deserve the rough contact of red cloth; this hand is fit to protect subjects, it deserves not to hold food given by another.

25. 'If therefore, gentle youth, through thy love for thy father thou desirest not thy paternal kingdom in thy generosity,—then at any rate thy choice must not be excused,—accepting forthwith one half of my kingdom.

26. 'If thou actest thus there will be no violence

---

[1] N*ri*popavi*s*ya? with ârsha Sandhi.
[2] Lohita*k*andana may mean 'saffron.'

shown to thine own people, and by the mere lapse of time imperial power at last flies for refuge to the tranquil mind; therefore be pleased to do me a kindness,—the prosperity of the good becomes very powerful, when aided by the good[1].

27. 'But if from thy pride of race thou dost not now feel confidence in me, then plunge with thy arrows into countless armies, and with me as thy ally seek to conquer thy foes.

28. 'Choose thou therefore one of these ends, pursue according to rule religious merit, wealth, and pleasure; for these, love and the rest, in reverse order, are the three objects in life; when men die they pass into dissolution as far as regards this world.

29. 'That which is pleasure when it has overpowered wealth and merit, is wealth when it has conquered merit and pleasure; so too it is merit, when pleasure and wealth fall into abeyance; but all would have to be alike abandoned, if thy desired end[2] were obtained.

30. 'Do thou therefore by pursuing the three objects of life, cause this beauty of thine to bear its fruit; they say that when the attainment of religion, wealth, and pleasure is complete in all its parts, then the end of man is complete.

31. 'Do not thou let these two brawny arms lie useless which are worthy to draw the bow; they are well fitted like Mândhâtri's to conquer the three worlds, much more the earth.

---

[1] [The Tibetan translates the fourth line, dam-pa-rnams dan beas-pas dam-pai dpal ,phel-lo,'by being with the good the prosperity of the good increases.' H. W.]

[2] Nirvâna.

32. 'I speak this to you out of affection,—not through love of dominion or through astonishment; beholding this mendicant-dress of thine, I am filled with compassion and I shed tears.

33. 'O thou who desirest the mendicant's stage of life, enjoy pleasures now; in due time, O thou lover of religion, thou shalt practise religion;—ere old age comes on and overcomes this thy beauty, well worthy of thy illustrious race.

34. 'The old man can obtain merit by religion; old age is helpless for the enjoyment of pleasures; therefore they say that pleasures belong to the young man, wealth to the middle-aged, and religion to the old.

35. 'Youth in this present world is the enemy of religion and wealth,—since pleasures, however we guard them, are hard to hold, therefore, wherever pleasures are to be found, there they seize them.

36. 'Old age is prone to reflection[1], it is grave and intent on remaining quiet; it attains unimpassionedness with but little effort, unavoidably, and for very shame.

37. 'Therefore having passed through the deceptive period of youth, fickle, intent on external objects, heedless, impatient, not looking at the distance,—they take breath like men who have escaped safe through a forest.

38. 'Let therefore this fickle time of youth first pass by, reckless and giddy,—our early years are the mark for pleasure, they cannot be kept from the power of the senses.

39. 'Or if religion is really thy one aim, then offer

---

[1] Vimarsayanti?

sacrifices,—this is thy family's immemorial custom, —climbing to highest heaven by sacrifices, even Indra, the lord of the winds, went thus to highest heaven.

40. 'With their arms pressed[1] by golden bracelets, and their variegated diadems resplendent with the light of gems, royal sages have reached the same goal by sacrifices which great sages reached by self-mortification.'

41. Thus spoke the monarch of the Magadhas, who spoke well and strongly like Indra[2]; but having heard it, the prince did not falter, (firm) like the mountain Kailâsa, having its many summits variegated (with lines of metals).

---

[1] Vidash/a; cf. sa*m*dash/a in Raghuv. XVI, 65.
[2] Valabhid, 'the smiter of the demon Vala.'

BOOK XI.

1. Being thus addressed by the monarch of the Magadhas, in a hostile speech with a friendly face,—self-possessed, unchanged, pure by family and personal purity, the son of *S*uddhodana thus made answer:

2. 'This is not to be called a strange thing for thee, born as thou art in the great family whose ensign is the lion[1]—that by thee of pure conduct, O lover of thy friends, this line of conduct should be adopted towards him who stands as one of thy friends.

3. 'Amongst the bad a friendship, worthy of their family, ceases to continue (and fades) like prosperity among the faint-hearted; it is only the good who keep increasing the old friendship of their ancestors by a new succession of friendly acts.

4. 'But those men who act unchangingly towards their friends in reverses of fortune, I esteem in my heart as true friends; who is not the friend of the prosperous man in his times of abundance?

5. 'So those who, having obtained riches in the world, employ them for the sake of their friends and religion,—their wealth has real solidity, and when it perishes it produces no pain at the end.

6. 'This thy determination concerning me, O king, is prompted by pure generosity and friendship[2];

---

[1] So the Tibetan explains harya*m*ka, seṅ-ges mċan-pai.
[2] The Sanskrit of this line is corrupt and does not scan. The

I will meet thee courteously with simple friendship;
I would not utter aught else in my reply.

7. 'I, having experienced the fear of old age and death, fly to this path of religion in my desire for liberation; leaving behind my dear kindred with tears in their faces,—still more then those pleasures which are the causes of evil.

8. 'I am not so afraid even of serpents nor of thunderbolts falling from heaven, nor of flames blown together by the wind, as I am afraid of these worldly objects.

9. 'These transient pleasures,—the robbers of our happiness and our wealth, and which float empty and like illusions through the world,—infatuate men's minds even when they are only hoped for,—still more when they take up their abode in the soul.

10. 'The victims of pleasure attain not to happiness even in the heaven of the gods, still less in the world of mortals; he who is athirst is never satisfied with pleasures, as the fire, the friend of the wind, with fuel.

11. 'There is no calamity in the world like pleasures,—people are devoted to them through delusion; when he once knows the truth and so fears evil, what wise man would of his own choice desire evil?

12. 'When they have obtained all the earth girdled by the sea, kings wish to conquer the other side of the great ocean; mankind are never satiated

---

Tibetan renders it as follows: khyod-kyi (te) ñes-pa (viniṣkayaḥ) gaṅ-zhig bdag-la dmigs-pa ˏdi, 'whatever a determination of thine imagines of me, to this (answering I would say).' I would read vibhāvya mām eva. The translation given above is conjectural.

with pleasures, as the ocean with the waters that fall into it.

13. 'When it had rained a golden shower from heaven, and when he had conquered the continents and the four oceans, and had even obtained the half of *S*akra's throne¹, Mândhât*ri* was still unsatisfied with worldly objects.

14. 'Though he had enjoyed the kingdom of the gods in heaven, when Indra had concealed himself through fear of V*ri*tra, and though in his pride he had made the great *Ri*shis bear his litter², Nahusha fell, unsatisfied with pleasures.

15. 'King (Purûravas) the son of I*d*â, having penetrated into the furthest heaven, and brought the goddess Urva*s*î into his power,—when he wished in his greed to take away gold from the *Ri*shis³,—being unsatisfied with pleasures, fell into destruction.

16. 'Who would put his trust in these worldly objects, whether in heaven or in earth, unsettled as to lot or family,—which passed from Bali to Indra, and from Indra to Nahusha, and then again from Nahusha back to Indra?

17. 'Who would seek these enemies bearing the name of pleasures, by whom even those sages have been overcome, who were devoted to other pursuits, whose only clothes were rags, whose food was roots, fruits, and water, and who wore their twisted locks as long as snakes?

18. 'Those pleasures for whose sake even Ugrâ-yudha⁴, armed terribly as he was with his weapon,

---

¹ Divyâvadâna, pp. 213-224.   ² Mahâbh. V, 532.
³ Mahâbh. I, 3147.
⁴ See Hariva*ms*a, ch. xx. He was armed with a discus.

found death at Bhishma's hands,—is not the mere thought of them unlucky and fatal,—still more the thought of the irreligious whose lives are spent in their service?

19. 'Who that considers the paltry flavour of worldly objects,—the very height of union being only insatiety,—the blame of the virtuous, and the certain sin,—has ever drawn near this poison which is called pleasure?

20. 'When they hear of the miseries of those who are intent on pleasure and are devoted to worldly pursuits[1], such as agriculture and the rest, and the self-content of those who are careless of pleasure,—it well befits the self-controlled to fling it away[2].

21. 'Success in pleasure is to be considered a misery in the man of pleasure, for he becomes intoxicated when his desired pleasures are attained; through intoxication he does what should not be done, not what should be done; and being wounded thereby he falls into a miserable end.

22. 'These pleasures which are gained and kept by toil,—which after deceiving leave you and return whence they came,—these pleasures which are but borrowed for a time[3], what man of self-control, if he is wise, would delight in them?

23. 'What man of self-control could find satisfaction in these pleasures which are like a torch of hay,—which excite thirst when you seek them and when you grasp them, and which they who abandon not keep only as misery[4]?

24. 'Those men of no self-control who are bitten by

---

[1] Dharmabhi*h*. (Cf. V, 5, 6.) [2] I would read kâmâ*h*.
[3] For yâ*k*itaka cf. Pâ*n*. IV, 4, 21. [4] I would read paripânti.

them in their hearts, fall into ruin and attain not bliss, —what man of self-control could find satisfaction in these pleasures, which are like an angry, cruel serpent?

25. 'Even if they enjoy them men are not satisfied, like dogs famishing with hunger over a bone,— what man of self-control could find satisfaction in these pleasures, which are like a skeleton composed of dry bones?

26. 'What man of self-control could find satisfaction in these pleasures which are like flesh that has been flung away, and which produce misery by their being held only in common with kings, thieves, water, and fire[1]?

27. 'What man of self-control could find satisfaction in these pleasures, which, like the senses[2], are destructive, and which bring calamity on every hand to those who abide in them, from the side of friends even more than from open enemies?

28. 'What man of self-control could find satisfaction in those pleasures, which are like the fruit that grows on the top of a tree,—which those who would leap up to reach fall down upon a mountain or into a forest, waters, or the ocean?

29. 'What man of self-control could find satisfaction in those pleasures, which are like snatching up a hot coal,—men never attain happiness, however they pursue them, increase them, or guard them?

30. 'What man of self-control could find satisfaction in those pleasures, which are like the enjoyments in a dream,—which are gained by their recipients after manifold pilgrimages and labours, and then perish in a moment?

---

[1] I.e. any one of these can seize them from us.   [2] Âyatana.

31. 'What man of self-control could find satisfaction in those pleasures which are like a spear¹, sword, or club,—for the sake of which the Kurus, the Vrishnis and the Amdhakas, the Maithilas and the Damdakas suffered destruction?

32. 'What man of self-control could find satisfaction in those pleasures which dissolve friendships and for the sake of which the two Asuras Sumda and Upasumda perished, victims engaged in mutual enmity?

33. 'None, however their intellect is blinded with pleasure, give themselves up, as in compassion, to ravenous beasts²; so what man of self-control could find satisfaction in those pleasures which are disastrous and constant enemies?

34. 'He whose intellect is blinded with pleasure does pitiable things; he incurs calamities, such as death, bonds, and the like; the wretch, who is the miserable slave of hope for the sake of pleasure, well deserves the pain of death even in the world of the living.

35. 'Deer are lured to their destruction by songs³, insects for the sake of the brightness fly into the fire, the fish greedy for the flesh swallows the iron hook,—therefore worldly objects produce misery as their end.

36. 'As for the common opinion, "pleasures are enjoyments," none of them when examined are

---

¹ The Chinese translation seems to take *sûla* as a stake for impaling criminals in ver. 864.

² The text is corrupt. I would read kravyâtsu nâtmânam. The va in line 1 is for iva, a rare form, but allowed by Sanskrit lexicographers. Perhaps we should translate kâmândhasamgña, 'these men who are called "blinded with pleasure."'

³ Cf. Kâdambari (Calc. ed.), p. 27, l. 6 infra.

worthy of being enjoyed; fine garments and the rest are only the accessories of things,—they are to be regarded as merely the remedies for pain.

37. 'Water is desired for allaying thirst; food in the same way for removing hunger; a house for keeping off the wind, the heat of the sun, and the rain; and dress for keeping off the cold and to cover one's nakedness.

38. 'So too a bed is for removing drowsiness; a carriage for remedying the fatigue of a journey; a seat for alleviating the pain of standing; so bathing as a means for washing, health, and strength.

39. 'External objects therefore are to human beings means for remedying pain, not in themselves sources of enjoyment; what wise man would allow that he enjoys those delights which are only used as remedial?

40. 'He who, when burned with the heat of bilious fever, maintains that cold appliances are an enjoyment, when he is only engaged in alleviating pain,— he indeed might give the name of enjoyment to pleasures.

41. 'Since variableness is found in all pleasures, I cannot apply to them the name of enjoyment; the very conditions which mark pleasure, bring also in its turn pain.

42. 'Heavy garments and fragrant aloe-wood are pleasant in the cold, but an annoyance in the heat[1]; and the moonbeams and sandal-wood are pleasant in the heat, but a pain in the cold.

43. 'Since the well-known opposite pairs[2], such

---

[1] I have adopted Professor Kielhorn's suggested reading sukhâya *s*îte hy asukhâya gharme.

[2] Cf. ἡ συστοιχία of the Pythagoreans (Arist. Ethics, I, 6).

as gain and loss and the rest, are inseparably connected with everything in this world,—therefore no man is invariably happy on the earth nor invariably wretched.

44. 'When I see how the nature of pleasure and pain are mixed, I consider royalty and slavery as the same; a king does not always smile, nor is a slave always in pain.

45. 'Since to be a king involves a wider range of command, therefore the pains of a king are great; for a king is like a peg[1],—he endures trouble for the sake of the world.

46. 'A king is unfortunate, if he places his trust in his royalty which is apt to desert and loves crooked turns[2]; and on the other hand, if he does not trust in it, then what can be the happiness of a timid king?

47. 'And since after even conquering the whole earth, one city only can serve as a dwelling-place, and even there only one house can be inhabited, is not royalty mere labour for others?

48. 'And even in royal clothing one pair of garments is all he needs, and just enough food to keep off hunger; so only one bed, and only one seat; all a king's other distinctions are only for pride.

49. 'And if all these fruits are desired for the sake of satisfaction, I can be satisfied without a kingdom; and if a man is once satisfied in this world, are not all distinctions indistinguishable?

50. 'He then who has attained the auspicious road to happiness is not to be deceived in regard to pleasures; remembering thy professed friendship, tell me again and again, do they keep their promise?

---

[1] Cf. Isaiah xxii. 23, 24 (יָתֵד).
[2] Professor Kielhorn would read ra*m*kamitre.

51. 'I have not repaired to the forest through anger, nor because my diadem has been dashed down by an enemy's arrows; nor have I set my desires on loftier objects[1], that I thus refuse thy proposal.

52. 'Only he who, having once let go a malignant incensed serpent, or a blazing hay-torch all on fire, would strive again to seize it, would ever seek pleasures again after having once abandoned them.

53. 'Only he who, though seeing, would envy the blind, though free the bound, though wealthy the destitute, though sound in his reason the maniac,—only he, I say, would envy one who is devoted to worldly objects.

54. 'He who lives on alms, my good friend, is not to be pitied, having gained his end and being set on escaping the fear of old age and death; he has here the best happiness, perfect calm, and hereafter all pains are for him abolished.

55. 'But he is to be pitied who is overpowered by thirst though set in the midst of great wealth,—who attains not the happiness of calm here, while pain has to be experienced hereafter.

56. 'Thus to speak to me is well worthy of thy character, thy mode of life, and thy family; and to carry out my resolve is also befitting my character, my mode of life, and my family.

57. 'I have been wounded by the enjoyment of the world, and I have come out longing to obtain peace; I would not accept an empire free from all ill even in the third heaven, how much less amongst men?

58. 'But as for what thou saidst to me, O king, that the universal pursuit of the three objects is the

---

[1] Sc. as rule in heaven, &c.

supreme end of man,—and[1] thou saidst that what I regard as the desirable is misery,—thy three objects are perishable and also unsatisfying.

59. 'But that world in which there is no old age nor fear, no birth, nor death, nor anxieties[2], that alone I consider the highest end of man, where there is no ever-renewed action.

60. 'And as for what thou saidst, "wait till old age comes, for youth is ever subject to change;"— this want of decision is itself uncertain; for age too can be irresolute and youth can be firm.

61. 'But since Fate[3] is so well skilled in its art as to draw the world in all its various ages into its power,—how shall the wise man, who desires tranquillity, wait for old age, when he knows not when the time of death will be?

62. 'When death stands ready like a hunter, with old age as his weapon, and diseases scattered about as his arrows, smiting down living creatures who fly like deer to the forest of destiny, what desire can there be in any one for length of life?

63. 'It well befits the youthful son or the old man or the child so to act with all promptitude that they may choose the action of the religious man whose soul is all mercy,—nay, better still, his inactivity.

64. 'And as for what thou saidst, "be diligent in sacrifices for religion, such as are worthy of thy race and bring a glorious fruit,"—honour to such sacrifices! I desire not that fruit which is sought by causing pain to others[4]!

---

[1] I would read anartha ity āttha (for ity artha).

[2] Ādhayaḥ.

[3] Ko, 'who?' seems here used for 'fate.' Professor Kielhorn would read—Yadāṁtako gagad vayaḥsu sarveshu vasaṁ vikarshati.

[4] Yad ishyate is the true reading.

65. 'To kill a helpless victim through a wish for future reward,—it would be an unseemly action for a merciful-hearted good man, even if the reward of the sacrifice were eternal; but what if, after all, it is subject to decay?

66. 'And even if true religion did not consist in quite another rule of conduct, by self-restraint, moral practice and a total absence of passion,—still it would not be seemly to follow the rule of sacrifice, where the highest reward is described as attained only by slaughter.

67. 'Even that happiness which comes to a man, while he stays in this world, through the injury of another, is hateful to the wise compassionate heart; how much more if it be something beyond our sight in another life?

68. 'I am not to be lured into a course of action for future reward,—my mind does not delight, O king, in future births; these actions are uncertain and wavering in their direction, like plants beaten by the rain from a cloud.

69. 'I have come here with a wish to see next the seer Arâ*d*a who proclaims liberation; I start this very day,—happiness be to thee, O king; forgive my words which may seem harsh through their absolute freedom from passion [1].

70. '[2] Now therefore do thou guard (the world) like Indra in heaven; guard it continually like the sun by thy excellencies; guard its best happiness here;

---

[1] I read *s*amatattva.
[2] This verse is obscure,—the division of the clauses is uncertain, the Chinese translation giving only six; but ava seems to occur eight times. The Tibetan has its equivalent sru*n*s nine times.

guard the earth; guard life by the noble[1]; guard the sons of the good; guard thy royal powers, O king; and guard thine own religion.

71. 'As in the midst of a sudden catastrophe arising from the flame of (fire), the enemy of cold, a bird, to deliver its body, betakes itself to the enemy of fire (water),—so do thou, when occasion calls, betake thyself, to deliver thy mind, to those who will destroy the enemies of thy home [2].'

72. The king himself, folding his hands, with a sudden longing come upon him, replied, 'Thou art obtaining thy desire without hindrance; when thou hast at last accomplished all that thou hast to do, thou shalt show hereafter thy favour towards me.'

73. Having given his firm promise to the monarch, he proceeded to the Vaisvamtara hermitage; and, after watching him with astonishment, as he wandered on in his course, the king and[3] his courtiers returned to the mountain (of Râgagiri).

---

[1] So the Tibetan.

[2] This is a very hard verse, but the obscure Chinese translation helps to explain it, vv. 912-915. I read in c, himârisatrum, i.e. water, as the enemy of the enemy of cold (fire). The bird flies to water to stop the effects of fire; as the king is to destroy his enemies by means of their enemies, cf. Manu VII, 158. Here, however, it seems to mean also that he is to destroy his passions by their opposites; the home (kshaya) is the summum bonum, nirvâna.—I read samplava for sambhava, as the two words are confused in XII, 24 and 28.

[3] Ka seems used in a very artificial manner with the ellipsis of the substantive which should follow it; cf. Amarakosha III, 4, 1, 6 (we might also read prâpad).

BOOK XII.

1. Then the moon of the Ikshvâku race turned towards the hermitage of the sage Arâda[1] of tranquil life,—as it were, doing honour to it by his beauty.

2. He drew near, on being addressed in a loud voice 'Welcome' by the kinsman of Kâlâma, as he saw him from afar.

3. They, having mutually asked after each other's health as was fitting, sat down in a clean place on two pure wooden seats.

4. The best of sages, having seen the prince seated, and as it were drinking in the sight of him with eyes opened wide in reverence, thus addressed him:

5. 'I know, gentle youth, how thou hast come forth from thy home, having severed the bond of affection, as a wild elephant its cord.

6. 'In every way thy mind is stedfast and wise, who hast come here after abandoning royal luxury like a creeper-plant with poisonous fruit.

7. 'It is no marvel that kings have retired to the forest who have grown old in years, having given up their glory to their children, like a garland left behind after being used.

8. 'But this is to me indeed a marvel that thou art come hither in life's fresh prime, set in the open field

---

[1] Arâda holds an early form of the Sâmkhya doctrine.

of the world's enjoyments, ere thou hast as yet tasted of their happiness.

9. 'Verily thou art a worthy vessel to receive this highest religion; having mastered it with full knowledge, cross at once over the sea of misery.

10. 'Though the doctrine is generally efficient only after a time, when the student has been thoroughly tested, thou art easy for me to examine from thy depth of character and determination.'

11. The prince, having heard these words of Arâ*d*a, was filled with great pleasure and thus made reply:

12. 'This extreme kindliness which thou showest to me, calmly passionless as thou art, makes me, imperfect as I am, seem even already to have attained perfection.

13. 'I feel at the sight of thee like one longing to see who finds a light,—like one wishing to journey, a guide,—or like one wishing to cross, a boat.

14. 'Wilt thou therefore deign to tell me that secret, if thou thinkest it should be told, whereby thy servant may be delivered from old age, death, and disease.'

15. Arâ*d*a, thus impelled by the noble nature of the prince, declared in a concise form the tenets of his doctrine:

16. 'O best of hearers, hear this our firmly-settled theory, how our mortal existence arises and how it revolves.

17. '"The evolvent" and "the evolute," birth, old age, and death,—know that this has been called the reality by us; do thou receive our words, O thou who art stedfast in thy nature.

18. 'But know, O thou who art deep in the search

into the nature of things, that the five elements[1], egoism, intellect, and "the unmanifested" are the "evolvents;"

19. 'But know that the "evolutes" consist of intellect, external objects[2], the senses, and the hands, feet, voice, anus, and generative organ, and also the mind.

20. 'There is also a something which bears the name kshetragña, from its knowledge of this "field" (kshetra or the body); and those who investigate the soul call the soul kshetragña.

21. 'Kapila with his disciple became the illuminated,—such is the tradition; and he, as the illuminated, with his son is now called here Pragâpati.

22. 'That which is born and grows old and is bound and dies,—is to be known as "the manifested," and "the unmanifested" is to be distinguished by its contrariety.

23. 'Ignorance, the merit or demerit of former actions, and desire are to be known as the causes of mundane existence; he who abides in the midst of this triad does not attain to the truth of things,—

24. 'From mistake[3], egoism, confusion, fluctuation, indiscrimination, false means, inordinate attachment, and gravitation.

25. 'Now "mistake" acts in a contrary manner, it does wrongly what it should do, and what it should think it thinks wrongly.

26. '"I say," "I know," "I go," "I am firmly

---

[1] These are the tanmâtrâni or subtile elements.
[2] Vishayân, corresponding to the gross elements. The intellect, buddhi, is both an evolver and an evolute.
[3] Should we read viparyayâd? Cf. Sâmkhya, aphor. III, 37.

fixed," it is thus that "egoism" shows itself here, O thou who art free from all egoism.

27. 'That state of mind is called "confusion," O thou who art all unconfused, which views under one nature, massed like a lump of clay, objects that thus become confused in their nature.

28. 'That state of mind which says that this mind, intellect, and these actions are the same as "I," and that which says that all this aggregate is the same as "I,"—is called "fluctuation."

29. 'That state of mind is called "indiscrimination," O thou who art discriminating, which thinks there is no difference between the illuminated and the unwise, and between the different evolvents.

30. 'Uttering "namas" and "vasha*t*," sprinkling water upon sacrifices, &c. with or without the recital of Vedic hymns, and such like rites,—these are declared by the wise to be "false means," O thou who art well skilled in true means.

31. 'That is called "inordinate attachment," by which the fool is entangled in external objects through his mind, speech, actions, and thoughts, O thou who hast shaken thyself free from all attachments.

32. 'The misery which a man imagines by the ideas "This is mine," "I am connected with this," is to be recognised as "gravitation,"—by this a man is borne downwards into new births.

33. 'Thus Ignorance, O ye wise, being fivefold in its character, energises towards torpor, delusion, the great delusion, and the two kinds of darkness[1].

34. 'Know, that among these indolence is "torpor," death and birth are "delusion," and be it clearly

---

[1] Cf. Sâ*m*khyakârikâ, 48.

understood, O undeluded one, that desire is the "great delusion."

35. 'Since by it even the higher beings are deluded, therefore, O hero, is this called the "great delusion."

36. 'They define anger, O thou angerless one, as "darkness;" and despondency, O undesponding, they pronounce to be the "blind darkness."

37. 'The child, entangled in this fivefold ignorance, is effused in his different births in a world abounding with misery.

38. 'He wanders about in the world of embodied existence, thinking that I am the seer, and the hearer, and the thinker,—the effect and the cause.

39. 'Through these causes[1], O wise prince, the stream of "torpor" is set in motion; be pleased to consider that in the absence of the cause there is the absence of the effect.

40. 'Let the wise man who has right views know these four things, O thou who desirest liberation,—the illuminated and the unilluminated, the manifested and the unmanifested.

41. 'The soul, having once learned to distinguish these four properly, having abandoned all (ideas of) straightness or quickness[2], attains to the immortal sphere.

42. 'For this reason the Brâhmans in the world, discoursing on the supreme Brahman, practise here a rigorous course of sacred study and let other Brâhmans live with them to follow it also.'

43. The prince, having heard this discourse from the seer, asked concerning the means and the final state.

---

[1] Cf. ver. 23.
[2] It rises above all relative ideas? The text may be corrupt.

44. 'Wilt thou please to explain to me how, how far, and where this life of sacred study is to be led, and the limit of this course of life[1]?'

45. Then Arâḍa, according to his doctrine, declared to him in another way that course of life clearly and succinctly.

46. 'The devotee, in the beginning, having left his house, and assumed the signs of the mendicant, goes on, following a rule of conduct which extends to the whole life.

47. 'Cultivating absolute content with any alms from any person, he carries out his lonely life, indifferent to all feelings, meditating on the holy books, and satisfied in himself.

48. 'Then having seen how fear arises from passion and the highest happiness from the absence of passion, he strives, by restraining all the senses, to attain to tranquillity of mind.

49. 'Then he reaches the first stage of contemplation, which is separated from desires, evil intentions and the like, and arises from discrimination and which involves reasoning[2].

50. 'And having obtained this ecstatic contemplation, and reasoning on various objects, the childish mind is carried away by the possession of the new unknown ecstasy.

51. 'With a tranquillity of this kind, which disdains desire or dislike, he reaches the world of Brahman, deceived by the delight.

52. 'But the wise man, knowing that these reasonings bewilder the mind, reaches a (second) stage of contemplation separate from this, which has its own pleasure and ecstasy.

---

[1] Dharma.   [2] Cf. Yoga-sûtras I, 42.

53. 'And he who, carried away by this pleasure, sees no further distinction, obtains a dwelling full of light, even amongst the Âbhâsura deities.

54. 'But he who separates his mind from this pleasure and ecstasy, reaches the third stage of contemplation ecstatic but without pleasure.

55. 'Upon this stage some teachers make their stand, thinking that it is indeed liberation, since pleasure and pain have been left behind and there is no exercise of the intellect.

56. 'But he who, immersed in this ecstasy, strives not for a further distinction, obtains an ecstasy in common with the Subhakr*i*tsna deities.

57. 'But he who, having attained such a bliss desires it not but despises it, obtains the fourth stage of contemplation which is separate from all pleasure or pain.

58. 'The fruit of this contemplation which is on an equality with the Vr*i*hatphala deities, those who investigate the great wisdom call the Vr*i*hatphala [1].

59. 'But rising beyond this contemplation, having seen the imperfections of all embodied souls, the wise man climbs to a yet higher wisdom in order to abolish all body.

60. 'Then, having abandoned this contemplation, being resolved to find a further distinction, he becomes as disgusted with form itself as he who knows the real is with pleasures.

61. 'First he makes use of all the apertures of his body; and next he exerts his will to experience a feeling of void space even in the solid parts [2].

62. 'But another wise man, having contracted his soul which is by nature extended everywhere like

---

[1] The great fruit.   [2] An obscure verse; cf. Pâli Dict.

the ether,[1]—as he gazes ever further on, detects a yet higher distinction.

63. 'Another one of those who are profoundly versed in the supreme Self, having abolished himself by himself, sees that nothing exists and is called a Nihilist[2].

64. 'Then like the Mu*n*ga-reed's stalk[3] from its sheath or the bird from its cage, the soul, escaped from the body, is declared to be "liberated."

65. 'This is that supreme Brahman, constant, eternal, and without distinctive signs; which the wise who know reality declare to be liberation.

66. 'Thus have I shown to thee the means and liberation; if thou hast understood and approved it, then act accordingly.

67. '*G*aigîshavya[4] and *G*anaka, and the aged Parâsara, by following this path, were liberated, and so were others who sought liberation.'

68. The prince having not accepted his words but having pondered them, filled with the force of his former arguments, thus made answer:

69. 'I have heard this thy doctrine, subtil and pre-eminently auspicious, but I hold that it cannot be final, because it does not teach us how to abandon this soul itself in the various bodies.

70. 'For I consider that the embodied soul, though freed from the evolutes and the evolvents, is still subject to the condition of birth and has the condition of a seed[5].

71. 'Even though the pure soul is declared to be

---

[1] Cf. Bhâshâparik*kh*eda, *s*loka 25.
[2] Âkim*k*anya.   [3] Cf. Ka*th*a Up. VI, 17.
[4] Mahâbh. IX, § 50; Tattvakaumudî, § 5.
[5] This is expanded in the Chinese, vv. 984, 985.

"liberated," yet as long as the soul remains there can be no absolute abandonment of it.

72. 'If we abandon successively all this triad, yet "distinction" is still perceived; as long as the soul itself continues, there this triad continues in a subtil form.

73. 'It is held (by some) that this is liberation, because the "imperfections" are so attenuated, and the thinking power is inactive, and the term of existence is so prolonged;

74. 'But as for this supposed abandonment of the principle of egoism,—as long as the soul continues, there is no real abandonment of egoism.

75. 'The soul does not become free from qualities as long as it is not released from number and the rest; therefore, as long as there is no freedom from qualities, there is no liberation declared for it.

76. 'There is no real separation of the qualities and their subject; for fire cannot be conceived, apart from its form and heat.

77. 'Before the body there will be nothing embodied, so before the qualities there will be no subject; how, if it was originally free, could the soul ever become bound[1]?

78. 'The body-knower (the soul) which is unembodied, must be either knowing or unknowing; if it is knowing, there must be some object to be known, and if there is this object, it is not liberated.

79. 'Or if the soul is declared to be unknowing, then of what use to you is this imagined soul? Even without such a soul, the existence of the absence of knowledge is notorious as, for instance, in a log of wood or a wall.

---

[1] I read kasmât for tasmât.

80. 'And since each successive abandonment is held to be still accompanied by qualities, I maintain that the absolute attainment of our end can only be found in the abandonment of everything.'

81. Thus did he remain unsatisfied after he had heard the doctrine of Arâḍa; then having decided it to be incomplete, he turned away.

82. Seeking to know the true distinction, he went to the hermitage of Udraka[1], but he gained no clear understanding from his treatment of the soul.

83. For the sage Udraka, having learned the inherent imperfections of the name and the thing named, took refuge in a theory beyond Nihilism, which maintained a name and a non-name.

84. And since even a name and a non-name were substrata, however subtil, he went even further still and found his restlessness set at rest in the idea that there is no named and no un-named;

85. And because the intellect rested there, not proceeding any further,—it became very subtil, and there was no such thing as un-named nor as named.

86. But because, even when it has reached this goal it yet returns again to the world, therefore the Bodhisattva, seeking something beyond, left Udraka.

87. Having quitted his hermitage, fully resolved in his purpose, and seeking final bliss, he next visited the hermitage, called a city, of the royal sage Gaya.

88. Then on the pure bank of the Nairañganâ the saint whose every effort was pure fixed his dwelling, bent as he was on a lonely habitation.

89. Five mendicants, desiring liberation, came

---

[1] Cf. Burnouf, Introd. p. 386 n. It is written Rudraka in XV, 89.

up to him when they beheld him there, just as the objects of the senses come up to a percipient who has gained wealth and health by his previous merit.

90. Being honoured by these disciples who were dwelling in that family, as they bowed reverently with their bodies bent low in humility, as the mind is honoured by the restless senses,

91. And thinking, 'this may be the means of abolishing birth and death,' he at once commenced a series of difficult austerities by fasting.

92. For six years, vainly trying to attain merit[1], he practised self-mortification, performing many rules of abstinence, hard for a man to carry out.

93. At the hours for eating, he, longing to cross the world whose farther shore is so difficult to reach, broke his vow with single jujube fruits, sesame seeds, and rice.

94. But the emaciation which was produced in his body by that asceticism, became positive fatness through the splendour which invested him.

95. Though thin, yet with his glory and his beauty unimpaired, he caused gladness to other eyes, as the autumnal moon in the beginning of her bright fortnight gladdens the lotuses.

96. Having only skin and bone remaining, with his fat, flesh and blood entirely wasted, yet, though diminished, he still shone with undiminished grandeur like the ocean.

97. Then the seer, having his body evidently emaciated to no purpose in a cruel self-mortifica-

---

[1] This is the Tibetan reading [las-ni thob-bzhed lo drug-tu. 'wishing to obtain (the fruits of good) works, during six years.' H.W.]

tion,—dreading continued existence, thus reflected in his longing to become a Buddha:

98. 'This is not the way to passionlessness, nor to perfect knowledge, nor to liberation; that was certainly the true way which I found at the root of the *G*ambu[1] tree.

99. 'But that cannot be attained by one who has lost his strength,'—so resuming his care for his body, he next pondered thus, how best to increase his bodily vigour:

100. 'Wearied with hunger, thirst, and fatigue, with his mind no longer self-possessed through fatigue, how should one who is not absolutely calm reach the end which is to be attained by his mind?

101. 'True calm is properly obtained by the constant satisfaction of the senses; the mind's self-possession is only obtained by the senses being perfectly satisfied.

102. 'True meditation is produced in him whose mind is self-possessed and at rest,—to him whose thoughts are engaged in meditation the exercise of perfect contemplation begins at once.

103. 'By contemplation are obtained those conditions[2] through which is eventually gained that supreme calm, undecaying, immortal state, which is so hard to be reached.'

104. Having thus resolved, 'this means is based upon eating food,' the wise seer of unbounded wisdom, having made up his mind to accept the continuance of life,

105. And having bathed, thin as he was, slowly

---

[1] The rose apple, see V, 8.   [2] Dharmâ*h*.

came up the bank of the Nairañganâ, supported as by a hand by the trees on the shore, which bent down the ends of their branches in adoration.

106. Now at that time Nandabalâ, the daughter of the leader of the herdsmen, impelled by the gods, with a sudden joy risen in her heart, had just come near,

107. Her arm gay with a white shell, and wearing a dark blue woollen cloth, like the river Yamunâ, with its dark blue water and its wreath of foam.

108. She, having her joy increased by her faith, with her lotus-like eyes opened wide, bowed down before him and persuaded him to take some milk.

109. By partaking that food having made her obtain the full reward of her birth, he himself became capable of gaining the highest knowledge, all his six senses being now satisfied,

110. The seer, having his body now fully robust, together with his glorious fame, one beauty and one majesty being equally spread in both, shone like the ocean and the moon[1].

111. Thinking that he had returned to the world the five mendicants left him, as the five elements leave the wise soul when it is liberated.

112. Accompanied only by his own resolve, having fixed his mind on the attainment of perfect knowledge, he went to the root of an Asvattha tree[2], where the surface of the ground was covered with young grass.

113. Then Kâla[3], the best of serpents, whose

---

[1] Fame is often compared for its brightness to the moon.
[2] Ficus religiosa or pipul tree.
[3] He is the Nâga king, Gâtaka I, 72.

majesty was like the lord of elephants, having been awakened by the unparalleled sound of his feet, uttered this praise of the great sage, being sure that he was on the point of attaining perfect knowledge:

114. 'Inasmuch as the earth, pressed down by thy feet, O sage, resounds repeatedly, and inasmuch as thy splendour shines forth like the sun, thou shalt assuredly to-day enjoy the desired fruit.

115. 'Inasmuch as lines of birds fluttering in the sky offer thee reverential salutation, O lotus-eyed one, and inasmuch as gentle breezes blow in the sky, thou shalt certainly to-day become the Buddha.'

116. Being thus praised by the best of serpents, and having taken some pure grass from a grass-cutter, he, having made his resolution, sat down to obtain perfect knowledge at the foot of the great holy tree.

117. Then he sat down on his hams in a posture, immovably firm and with his limbs gathered into a mass like a sleeping serpent's hood, exclaiming, 'I will not rise from this position on the earth [1] until I have obtained my utmost aim.'

118. Then the dwellers in heaven burst into unequalled joy; the herds of beasts and the birds uttered no cry; the trees moved by the wind made no sound, when the holy one took his seat firm in his resolve.

---

[1] For tâvat read yâvat.

BOOK XIII.

1. When the great sage, sprung from a line of royal sages, sat down there with his soul fully resolved to obtain the highest knowledge, the whole world rejoiced; but Mâra, the enemy of the good law, was afraid.

2. He whom they call in the world Kâmadeva, the owner of the various weapons, the flower-arrowed, the lord of the course of desire,—it is he whom they also style Mâra the enemy of liberation.

3. His three sons, Confusion, Gaiety, and Pride, and his three daughters, Lust, Delight, and Thirst[1], asked of him the reason of his despondency, and he thus made answer unto them:

4. 'This sage, wearing the armour of resolution, and having drawn the arrow of wisdom with the barb of truth, sits yonder intending to conquer my realms,—hence is this despondency of my mind.

5. 'If he succeeds in overcoming me and proclaims to the world the path of final bliss, all this my realm will to-day become empty, as did that of the disembodied lord when he violated the rules of his station[2].

6. 'While, therefore, he stands within my reach

---

[1] For these cf. also ver. 14, and XV, 13.

[2] This probably refers to the legend of Nimi-videha, see Vish*n*u Pur. IV, 5; it might be 'the king of the Videhas.' There may be also a secondary allusion to the legend of Ananga and *S*iva.

and while his spiritual eyesight is not yet attained, I will assail him to break his vow as the swollen might of a river assails a dam.'

7. Then having seized his flower-made bow and his five infatuating arrows, he drew near to the root of the A*s*vattha tree with his children, he the great disturber of the minds of living beings.

8. Having fixed his left hand on the end of the barb and playing with the arrow, Mâra thus addressed the calm seer as he sat on his seat, preparing to cross to the further side of the ocean of existence:

9. 'Up, up, O thou Kshatriya, afraid of death! follow thine own duty and abandon this law of liberation! and having conquered the lower worlds by thy arrows, proceed to gain the higher worlds of Indra.

10. 'That is a glorious path to travel, which has been followed by former leaders of men; this mendicant life is ill-suited for one born in the noble family of a royal sage to follow.

11. 'But if thou wilt not rise, strong in thy purpose,—then be firm if thou wilt and quit not thy resolve,—this arrow is uplifted by me,—it is the very one which was shot against Sûryaka[1], the enemy of the fish.

12. 'So too, I think, when somewhat probed by this weapon, even the son of I*d*â[2], the grandson of the moon, became mad; and Sâ*m*tanu[3] also lost

---

[1] The sun, alluding to his amour with Va*d*avâ. (The lake is called vipannaminam in *R*itusa*m*hâra I, 20.)

[2] Purûravas. (Professor Bühler suggests spri*sh*ta*h*.)

[3] Does this mean Vi*k*itravîrya the grandson of Sa*m*tanu, see Vish*n*u Pur. IV, 20?

his self-control, — how much more then one of feebler powers now that the age has grown degenerate?

13. 'Therefore quickly rise up and come to thyself,—for this arrow is ready, darting out its tongue, which I do not launch even against the *k*akravâka birds, tenderly attached as they are and well deserving the name of lovers.'

14. But when, even though thus addressed, the *S*âkya saint unheeding did not change his posture, then Mâra discharged his arrow at him, setting in front of him his daughters and his sons [1].

15. But even when that arrow was shot he gave no heed and swerved not from his firmness; and Mâra, beholding him thus, sank down, and slowly thus spoke, full of thought:

16. 'He does not even notice that arrow by which the god *S*ambhu was pierced with love for the daughter of the mountain [2] and shaken in his vow; can he be destitute of all feeling? is not this that very arrow?

17. 'He is not worthy of my flower-shaft, nor my arrow "gladdener," nor the sending of my daughter Rati (to tempt him); he deserves the alarms and rebukes and blows from all the gathered hosts of the demons.'

18. Then Mâra called to mind his own army, wishing to work the overthrow of the *S*âkya saint; and his followers swarmed round, wearing different forms and carrying arrows, trees, darts, clubs, and swords in their hands;

19. Having the faces of boars, fishes, horses, asses,

---

[1] See ver. 3.   [2] Umâ.

and camels, of tigers, bears, lions, and elephants,—one-eyed, many-faced, three-headed,—with protuberant bellies and speckled bellies;

20. Blended with goats, with knees swollen like pots, armed with tusks and with claws, carrying headless trunks in their hands, and assuming many forms, with half-mutilated faces, and with monstrous mouths;

21. Copper-red, covered with red spots, bearing clubs in their hands, with yellow or smoke-coloured hair, with wreaths dangling down, with long pendulous ears like elephants, clothed in leather or wearing no clothes at all;

22. Having half their faces white or half their bodies green,—red and smoke-coloured, yellow and black,—with arms reaching out longer than a serpent, and with girdles jingling with rattling bells.

23. Some were as tall as palm-trees, carrying spears,—others were of the size of children with projecting teeth, others birds with the faces of rams, others with men's bodies and cats' faces;

24. With dishevelled hair, or with topknots, or half-bald, with rope-garments or with head-dress all in confusion,—with triumphant faces or frowning faces,—wasting the strength or fascinating the mind.

25. Some as they went leaped about wildly, others danced upon one another, some sported about in the sky, others went along on the tops of the trees.

26. One danced, shaking a trident, another made a crash, dragging a club, another bounded for joy like a bull, another blazed out flames from every hair.

27. Such were the troops of demons who encircled the root of the Bodhi tree on every side, eager to

seize it and to destroy it, awaiting the command of their lord.

28. Beholding in the first half of the night that battle of Mâra and the bull of the Sâkya race, the heavens did not shine and the earth shook and the (ten) regions of space flashed flames and roared.

29. A wind of intense violence blew in all directions[1], the stars did not shine, the moon gave no light, and a deeper darkness of night spread around, and all the oceans were agitated.

30. The mountain deities[2] and the Nâgas who honoured the Law, indignant at the attack on the saint, rolling their eyes in anger against Mâra, heaved deep sighs and opened their mouths wide.

31. But the god-sages, the Suddhâdhivâsas[3], being as it were absorbed in the perfect accomplishment of the good Law, felt only a pity for Mâra in their minds and through their absolute passionlessness were unruffled by anger.

32. When they saw the foot of the Bodhi tree crowded with that host of Mâra, intent on doing harm,—the sky was filled with the cry raised by all the virtuous beings who desired the world's liberation.

33. But the great sage[4] having beheld that army of Mâra thus engaged in an attack on the knower of the Law[5], remained untroubled and suffered no perturbation, like a lion seated in the midst of oxen.

---

[1] Visvak should be corrected vishvak.

[2] Mahîbhritah. This might mean simply 'the rulers of the earth.'

[3] In Pâli Suddhâvâsâ. Cf. III, 26.

[4] Buddha himself, viewing all this ab extra.

[5] The Tibetan seems to read dharmavidheh for dharmavidah, as it has chos-kyi cho-ga de-ni, '(injurer) of that law of dharma.'

34. Then Mâra commanded his excited army of demons to terrify him; and forthwith that host resolved to break down his determination with their various powers.

35. Some with many tongues hanging out and shaking, with sharp-pointed savage teeth and eyes like the disk of the sun, with wide-yawning mouths and upright ears like spikes,—they stood round trying to frighten him.

36. Before these monsters standing there, so dreadful in form and disposition, the great sage remained unalarmed and untroubled, sporting with them as if they had been only rude children [1].

37. Then one of them, with his eyes rolling wildly, lifted up a club against him; but his arm with the club was instantly paralysed, as was Indra's of old with its thunderbolt [2].

38. Some, having lifted up stones and trees, found themselves unable to throw them against the sage; down they fell, with their trees and their stones, like the roots of the Vindhya shattered by the thunderbolt.

39. Others, leaping up into the sky, flung rocks, trees, and axes; these remained in the sky and did not fall down, like the many-coloured rays of the evening clouds.

40. Another hurled upon him a mass of blazing straw as big as a mountain-peak, which, as soon as it was thrown, while it hung poised in the sky, was shattered into a hundred fragments by the sage's power.

41. One, rising up like the sun in full splendour, rained down from the sky a great shower of live

---

[1] Prof. Bühler suggests svabâlebhya*h*, 'as with his own tossed hair.'
[2] Cf. Satap. Br. XII, 7, 3; Vish*n*u Pur. V, 30; Kum. Sambh. II, 20.

embers, as at the end of an aeon blazing Meru showers down the pulverised scoriae of the golden valleys.

42. But that shower of embers full of sparks, when scattered at the foot of the Bodhi tree, became a shower of red lotus-petals through the operation of the great saint's boundless charity.

43. But with all these various scorching assaults on his body and his mind, and all these missiles showered down upon him, the *S*âkya saint did not in the least degree move from his posture, clasping firmly his resolution as a kinsman.

44. Then others spat out serpents from their mouths as from old decayed trunks of trees; but, as if held fast by a charm, near him they neither breathed nor discharged venom nor moved.

45. Others, having become great clouds, emitting lightning and uttering the fierce roar of thunderbolts, poured a shower of stones upon that tree,—but it turned to a pleasant shower of flowers.

46. Another set an arrow in his bow,—there it gleamed but it did not issue forth, like the anger which falls slack[1] in the soul of an ill-tempered impotent man.

47. But five arrows shot by another stood motionless and fell not, through the saint's ruling guidance, —like the five senses of him who is well experienced in the course of worldly objects and is afraid of embodied existence.

48. Another, full of anger, rushed towards the great saint, having seized a club with a desire to

---

[1] Dhûryamâ*n*o is a difficult word, connected with √dh*v*rí or √dhûrv.

smite him; but he fell powerless without finding an opportunity, like mankind in the presence of faults which cause failure [1].

49. But a woman named Meghakâlî, bearing a skull in her hand, in order to infatuate the mind of the sage, flitted about unsettled and stayed not in one spot, like the mind of the fickle student over the sacred texts.

50. Another, fixing a kindling eye, wished to burn him with the fire of his glance like a poisonous serpent; but he saw the sage and lo! he was not there, like the votary of pleasure when true happiness is pointed out to him [2].

51. Another, lifting up a heavy rock, wearied himself to no purpose, having his efforts baffled,—like one who wishes to obtain by bodily fatigue that condition of supreme happiness which is only to be reached by meditation and knowledge.

52. Others, wearing the forms of hyenas and lions, uttered loudly fierce howls, which caused all beings round to quail with terror, as thinking that the heavens were smitten with a thunderbolt and were bursting.

53. Deer and elephants uttering cries of pain ran about or lay down,—in that night as if it were day screaming birds flew around disturbed in all directions.

54. But amidst all these various sounds which they made, although all living creatures were shaken, the saint trembled not nor quailed, like Garu*d*a at the noise of crows.

---

[1] Cf. randhropanipâtino·narthâ*h*, *S*akunt. VI.
[2] He had not eyes to see the object which he looked for.

55. The less the saint feared the frightful hosts of that multitude, the more did Mâra, the enemy of the righteous, continue his attacks in grief and anger.

56. Then some being of invisible shape, but of pre-eminent glory, standing in the heavens,—beholding Mâra thus malevolent against the seer,—addressed him in a loud voice, unruffled by enmity:

57. 'Take not on thyself, O Mâra, this vain fatigue,—throw aside thy malevolence and retire to peace[1]; this sage cannot be shaken by thee any more than the mighty mountain Meru by the wind.

58. 'Even fire might lose its hot nature, water its fluidity, earth its steadiness, but never will he abandon his resolution, who has acquired his merit by a long course of actions through unnumbered aeons.

59. 'Such is that purpose of his, that heroic effort, that glorious strength, that compassion for all beings,—until he attains the highest wisdom, he will never rise from his seat, just as the sun does not rise, without dispelling the darkness.

60. 'One who rubs the two pieces of wood obtains the fire, one who digs the earth finds at last the water,—and to him in his perseverance there is nothing unattainable,—all things to him are reasonable and possible.

61. 'Pitying the world lying distressed amidst diseases and passions, he, the great physician, ought not to be hindered, who undergoes all his labours for the sake of the remedy knowledge.

62. 'He who toilsomely pursues the one good path, when all the world is carried away in devious

---

[1] Or 'go to thy home.'

tracks,—he the guide should not be disturbed, like a right informant when the caravan has lost its way.

63. 'He who is made a lamp of knowledge when all beings are lost in the great darkness,—it is not for a right-minded soul to try to quench him,—like a lamp kindled in the gloom of night.

64. 'He who, when he beholds the world drowned in the great flood of existence and unable to reach the further shore, strives to bring them safely across,—would any right-minded soul offer him wrong?

65. 'The tree of knowledge, whose roots go deep in firmness, and whose fibres are patience,—whose flowers are moral actions and whose branches are memory and thought,—and which gives out the law as its fruit,—surely when it is growing it should not be cut down.

66. 'Him whose one desire is to deliver mankind bound in soul by the fast snares of illusion,—thy wish to overthrow him is not worthy, wearied as he is for the sake of unloosing the bonds of the world.

67. 'To-day is the appointed period of all those actions which have been performed by him for the sake of knowledge,—he is now seated on this seat just as all the previous saints have sat.

68. 'This is the navel of the earth's surface, endued with all the highest glory; there is no other spot of the earth than this,—the home of contemplation, the realm of well-being.

69. 'Give not way, then, to grief but put on calm; let not thy greatness, O Mâra, be mixed with pride; it is not well to be confident,—fortune

is unstable,—why dost thou accept a position on a tottering base?'

70. Having listened to his words, and having seen the unshaken firmness of the great saint, Mâra departed dispirited and broken in purpose[1] with those very arrows by which, O world, thou art smitten in thy heart.

71. With their triumph at an end, their labour all fruitless, and all their stones, straw, and trees thrown away, that host of his fled in all directions, like some hostile army when its camp has been destroyed by the enemy.

72. When the flower-armed god[2] thus fled away vanquished with his hostile forces and the passionless sage remained victorious, having conquered all the power of darkness, the heavens shone out with the moon like a maiden with a smile, and a sweet-smelling shower of flowers fell down wet with dew.

73. [3] When the wicked one thus fled vanquished, the different regions of the sky grew clear, the moon shone forth, showers of flowers fell down from the sky upon the earth, and the night gleamed out like a spotless maiden[4].

---

[1] I read hatodyamo.
[2] Mâra as identified with Kâmadeva, cf. ver. 2.
[3] Should we read tathâ hi for tathâpi?
[4] Here the original work of Asvaghosha ends according to the gloss at the close of the Cambridge MS. C; the four remaining books were added, to supply an old lacuna, by Amrıânanda, a modern Nepalese author. The Chinese and Tibetan translations seem to agree with the Sanskrit for part of the fourteenth book, but they soon diverge widely from it. The four books are included in the translation as a literary curiosity.

BOOK XIV.

1. Then, having conquered the hosts of Mâra by his firmness and calmness, he the great master of meditation set himself to meditate, longing to know the supreme end.

2. And having attained the highest mastery in all kinds of meditation, he remembered in the first watch the continuous series of all his former births.

3. 'In such a place I was so and so by name, and from thence I passed and came hither,' thus he remembered his thousands of births, experiencing each as it were over again.

4. And having remembered each birth and each death in all those various transmigrations, the compassionate one then felt compassion for all living beings.

5. Having wilfully rejected the good guides in this life and done all kinds of actions in various lives, this world of living beings rolls on helplessly, like a wheel.

6. As he thus remembered, to him in his strong self-control came the conviction, 'All existence is unsubstantial, like the fruit of a plantain.'

7. When the second watch came, he, possessed of unequalled energy, received a pre-eminent divine sight, he the highest of all sight-gifted beings.

8. Then by that divine perfectly pure sight he beheld the whole world as in a spotless mirror.

9. As he saw the various transmigrations and rebirths of the various beings with their several lower or higher merits from their actions, compassion grew up more within him.

10. 'These living beings, under the influence of evil actions, pass into wretched worlds,—these others, under the influence of good actions, go forward in heaven.

11. 'The one, being born in a dreadful hell full of terrors, are miserably tortured, alas! by many kinds of suffering;

12. 'Some are made to drink molten iron of the colour of fire, others are lifted aloft screaming on a red-hot iron pillar;

13. 'Others are baked like flour, thrown with their heads downwards into iron jars; others are miserably burned in heaps of heated charcoal;

14. 'Some are devoured by fierce dreadful dogs with iron teeth, others by gloating crows with iron beaks and all made as it were of iron;

15. 'Some, wearied of being burned, long for cold shade; these enter like bound captives into a dark blue wood with swords for leaves.

16. 'Others having many arms are split like timber with axes, but even in that agony they do not die, being supported in their vital powers by their previous actions.

17. 'Whatever deed was done only to hinder pain with the hope that it might bring pleasure, its result is now experienced by these helpless victims as simple pain.

18. 'These who did something evil for the sake

of pleasure and are now grievously pained,—does that old taste produce even an atom of pleasure to them now?

19. 'The wicked deed which was done by the wicked-hearted in glee,—its consequences are reaped by them in the fulness of time with cries.

20. 'If only evil doers could see the fruits of their actions, they would vomit hot blood as if they were smitten in a vital part.

21. 'And worse still than all these bodily tortures in hell seems to me the association of an intelligent man with the base.

22. 'Others also, through various actions arising from the spasmodic violence of their minds, are born miserable in the wombs of various beasts.

23. 'There the poor wretches are killed even in the sight of their kindred, for the sake of their flesh, their skin, their hair, or their teeth, or through hatred or for mere pleasure.

24. 'Even though powerless and helpless, oppressed by hunger, thirst, and fatigue, they are driven along as oxen and horses, their bodies wounded with goads.

25. 'They are driven along, when born as elephants, by weaker creatures than themselves for all their strength,—their heads tormented by the hook and their bodies kicked by foot and heel.

26. 'And with all these other miseries there is an especial misery arising from mutual enmity and from subjection to a master.

27. 'Air-dwellers are oppressed by air-dwellers, the denizens of water by the denizens of water, those that dwell on dry land are made to suffer by the dwellers on dry land in mutual hostility.

28. 'And others there are who, when born again, with their minds filled with envy, reap the miserable fruit of their actions in a world of the Pit*ri*s destitute of all light;

29. 'Having mouths as small as the eye of a needle and bellies as big as a mountain, these miserable wretches are tortured with the pains of hunger and thirst.

30. 'If a man only knew that such was the consequence of selfishness, he would always give to others even pieces of his own body like *S*ibi.

31. 'Rushing up filled with hope but held back by their former deeds, they try in vain to eat anything large, however impure.

32. 'Others, having found a hell in an impure lake called the womb, are born amongst men and there suffer anguish.

33. 'Others, ascetics, who have performed meritorious actions go to heaven; others, having attained widely extended empire, wander about on the earth[1];

34. 'Others as Nâgas in the subterranean regions become the guardians of treasures,—they wander in the ocean of existence, receiving the fruits of their deeds.'

35. Having pondered all this, in the last watch he thus reflected, 'Alas for this whole world of living beings doomed to misery, all alike wandering astray!

36. 'They know not that all this universe, destitute of any real refuge, is born and decays through that existence which is the site of the skandhas and pain;

---

[1] Heaven and earthly empire are alike transient.

37. 'It dies and passes into a new state and then is born anew.' Then he reflected, 'What is that which is the necessary condition for old age and death?'

38. He saw that when there is birth, there is old age and death, then he pondered, 'What is that which is the necessary condition for a new birth[1]?'

40. He perceived that where there has been the attachment to existence[2] there arises a (previous) existence; then he pondered, 'What is that which is the necessary condition for the attachment to existence?'

41. Having ascertained this to be desire, he again meditated, and he next pondered, 'What is that which is the necessary condition for desire?'

42. He saw that desire arises where there is sensation, and he next pondered, 'What is that which is the necessary condition for sensation?'

43. He saw that sensation arises where there is contact[3], and he next pondered, 'What is that which is the necessary condition for contact?'

44. He saw that contact arises through the six organs of sense; he then pondered, 'Where do the six organs of sense arise?'

45. He reflected that these arise in the organism[4], he then pondered, 'Where does the organism arise?'

---

[1] A verse (39) is omitted here containing the third step bhava (cf. Chinese translation, 1150, 1151), 'He perceived that when there has been a (previous) existence [involving previous actions] there is a new birth; then he pondered, "What is that which is the necessary condition for a previous existence arising?"' (Cf. Burnouf, Introd. pp. 485-506; Childers in Colebrooke's Essays, vol. i, 1873.)

[2] Upâdânam.   [3] Sc. between the senses and their objects.

[4] Nâmarûpa, sc. 'name and form,' i.e. the individual consisting of mind and body, as the embryo in the womb.

46. He saw that the organism arises where there is incipient consciousness; he then pondered, 'Where does incipient consciousness arise?'

47. He reflected that incipient consciousness arises where there are the latent impressions left by former actions; and he next pondered, 'Where do the latent impressions arise?'

48. He reflected exhaustively that they arise in ignorance; thus did the great seer, the Bodhisattva, the lord of saints,

49. After reflecting, pondering, and meditating, finally determine, 'The latent impressions start into activity after they are once developed from ignorance.

50. 'Produced from the activity of the latent impressions incipient consciousness starts into action; (the activity) of the organism starts into action on having an experience[1] of incipient consciousness;

51. 'The six organs of sense become active when produced in the organism; sensation is produced from the contact of the six organs (with their objects);

52. 'Desire starts into activity when produced from sensation; the attachment to existence springs from desire; from this attachment arises a (continued) existence;

53. 'Birth is produced where there has been a (continued) existence; and from birth arise old age, disease, and the rest; and scorched by the flame of old age and disease the world is devoured by death;

54. 'When it is thus scorched by the fire of

---

[1] Samparîkshya is a doubtful reading; I supply vrittih with nâmarûpasya.

death's anguish great pain arises; such verily is the origin of this great trunk of pain.'

55. Thus having ascertained it all, the great Being was perfectly illuminated; and having again meditated and pondered, he thus reflected,

56. 'When old age and disease are stopped, death also is stopped; and when birth is stopped, old age and disease are stopped;

57. 'When the action of existence is stopped, birth also is stopped; when the attachment to existence is stopped, the action of existence is stopped;

58. 'So too when desire is stopped, the attachment to existence is stopped; and with the stopping of sensation desire is no longer produced;

59. 'And when the contact of the six organs is stopped, sensation is no longer produced; and with the stopping of the six organs their contact (with their objects) is stopped;

60. 'And with the stopping of the organism the six organs are stopped; and with the stopping of incipient consciousness the organism is stopped;

61. 'And with the stopping of the latent impressions incipient consciousness is stopped; and with the stopping of ignorance the latent impressions have no longer any power.

62. 'Thus ignorance is declared to be the root of this great trunk of pain by all the wise; therefore it is to be stopped by those who seek liberation.

63. 'Therefore by the stopping of ignorance all the pains also of all existing beings are at once stopped and cease to act.'

64. The all-knowing Bodhisattva, the illuminated one, having thus determined, after again pondering and meditating thus came to his conclusion:

65. 'This is pain, this also is the origin of pain in the world of living beings; this also is the stopping of pain; this is that course which leads to its stopping.' So having determined he knew all as it really was.

66. Thus he, the holy one, sitting there on his seat of grass at the root of the tree, pondering by his own efforts attained at last perfect knowledge.

67. Then bursting the shell of ignorance, having gained all the various kinds of perfect intuition, he attained all the partial knowledge of alternatives which is included in perfect knowledge [1].

68. He became the perfectly wise, the Bhagavat, the Arhat, the king of the Law, the Tathâgata, He who has attained the knowledge of all forms, the Lord of all science.

69. Having beheld all this, the spirits standing in heaven spoke one to another, 'Strew flowers on this All-wise Monarch of Saints.'

70. While other immortals exclaimed, who knew the course of action of the greatest among the former saints, 'Do not now strew flowers—no reason for it has been shown.'

71. Then the Buddha, mounted on a throne, up in the air to the height of seven palm-trees, addressed all those Nirmitâ Bodhisattvâ*h* [2], illumining their minds,

72. 'Ho! ho! listen ye to the words of me who have now attained perfect knowledge; everything is achieved by meritorious works, therefore as long as existence lasts [3] acquire merit.

---

[1] Doubtful. I suppose it means that he knew all hypothetical as well as categorical propositions.

[2] These Nirmitâ Bodhisattvâ*h* seem to be the nimmâ*n*aratî devâ of the southern Buddhists with their nimmitâ kâmâ or self-created pleasures.

[3] Âbhavam.

73. 'Since I ever acted as liberal, pure-hearted, patient, skilful, devoted to meditation and wisdom,—by these meritorious works I became a Bodhisattva.

74. 'After accomplishing in due order the entire round of the preliminaries of perfect wisdom,—I have now attained that highest wisdom and I am become the All-wise Arhat and *G*ina.

75. 'My aspiration is thus fulfilled; this birth of mine has borne its fruit; the blessed and immortal knowledge which was attained by former Buddhas, is now mine.

76. 'As they through the good Law achieved the welfare of all beings, so also have I; all my sins are abolished, I am the destroyer of all pains.

77. 'Possessing a soul now of perfect purity, I urge all living beings to seek the abolition of worldly existence through the lamps of the Law.' Having worshipped him as he thus addressed them, those sons of the *G*inas disappeared.

78. The gods then with exultation paid him worship and adoration with divine flowers; and all the world, when the great saint had become all-wise, was full of brightness.

79. Then the holy one descended and stood on his throne under the tree; there he passed seven days filled with the thought, 'I have here attained perfect wisdom.'

80. When the Bodhisattva had thus attained perfect knowledge, all beings became full of great happiness; and all the different universes were illumined by a great light.

81. The happy earth shook in six different ways like an overjoyed woman, and the Bodhisattvas, each

dwelling in his own special abode, assembled and praised him.

82. 'There has arisen the greatest of all beings, the Omniscient All-wise Arhat—a lotus, unsoiled by the dust of passion, sprung up from the lake of knowledge;

83. 'A cloud bearing the water of patience, pouring forth the ambrosia of the good Law, fostering all the seeds of merit, and causing all the shoots of healing to grow;

84. 'A thunderbolt with a hundred edges, the vanquisher of Mâra, armed only with the weapon of patience; a gem fulfilling all desires, a tree of paradise, a jar of true good fortune [1], a cow that yields all that heart can wish;

85. 'A sun that destroys the darkness of delusion, a moon that takes away the scorching heat of the inherent sins of existence,—glory to thee, glory to thee, glory to thee, O Tathâgata;

86. 'Glory to thee, O Lord of the whole world, glory to thee, who hast gone through the ten (Balas [2]); glory to thee, O true hero amongst men, O Lord of righteousness, glory to thee!'

87. Thus having praised, honoured, and adored him, they each returned to their several homes, after making repeated reverential circumambulations, and recounting his eulogy.

88. Then the beings of the Kâmâva*k*ara worlds, and the brilliant inhabitants of the Pure Abodes, the

---

[1] The bhadrakumbha was the golden jar filled with consecrated water, used especially at the inauguration of a king.

[2] The ten balas are ten kinds of spiritual knowledge peculiar to a Buddha; but 'the ten' may be the ten dharmas, see Childers.

Brahmakâyika gods, and those sons of Mâra who favoured the side of truth[1],

89. The Paranirmitava*s*avarti beings, and the Nirmâ*n*aratayа*h*; the Tushita beings, the Yâmas, the Trayastri*m*sad Devas, and the other rulers of worlds,

90. The deities who roam in the sky, those who roam on the earth or in forests, accompanying each their own king, came to the pavilion of the Bodhi tree,

91. And having worshipped the *G*ina with forms of homage suitable to their respective positions, and having praised him with hymns adapted to their respective degrees of knowledge, they returned to their own homes.

---

[1] These terms are all explained in Childers' Dict. sattaloko. For the better-inclined sons of Mâra, cf. the dialogue between those of the right side and the left side before Mâra in the Lalitav. XXI, cf. also XXIII.

BOOK XV.

1. Daily praised by all the various heavenly beings, the perfectly Wise One [1] thus passed that period of seven days which is designated 'the aliment of joy [2].'

2. He then passed the second week, while he was bathed with jars full of water by the heavenly beings, the Bodhisattvas and the rest.

3. Then having bathed in the four oceans and being seated on his throne, he passed the third week restraining his eyes from seeing.

4. In the fourth week, assuming many forms, he stood triumphant on his throne, having delivered a being who was ready to be converted.

5. A god named Samamtakusuma, bearing an offering of flowers, thus addressed with folded hands the great Buddha who was seated there:

6. 'What is the name, O holy one, of this meditation, engaged in which thou hast thus passed four whole weeks with joy, deeply pondering?'

7. 'This is designated, O divine being, "the array [3] of the aliment of great joy," like an inaugurated king, who has overcome his enemies and enjoys prosperity.'

8. Having said this, the saint possessing the ten

---

[1] Sambuddha.

[2] Prîtyâhâra; this book corresponds closely with Lalitav. XXIV.

[3] Vyûha.

pre-eminent powers, full of joy, continued, 'The former perfect Buddhas also did not leave the Bodhi tree.

9. 'Here the Kle*s*as and the Mâras together with ignorance and the Âsravas have been conquered by me; and perfect wisdom has been attained able to deliver the world.

10. 'I too, resolved to follow the teaching of the former Buddhas, remained four whole weeks in the fulfilment of my inauguration[1].'

11. Then Mâra, utterly despondent in soul, thus addressed the Tathâgata, 'O holy one, be pleased to enter Nirvâ*n*a, thy desires are accomplished.'

12. 'I will first establish in perfect wisdom worlds as numerous as the sand, and then I will enter Nirvâ*n*a,' thus did the Buddha reply, and with a shriek Mâra went to his home.

13. Then the three daughters of Mâra, Lust, Thirst, and Delight[2], beholding their father with defeated face, approached the Tathâgata.

14. Lust, with a face like the moon and versed in all the arts of enchantment, tried to infatuate him by her descriptions of the pleasures of a householder's life.

15. 'Think, "If I abandon an emperor's happiness, with what paltry happiness shall I have to content myself? When success is lost, what shall I have to enjoy?"—and come and take refuge with us.

16. 'Else, in bitter repentance, thou wilt remember me hereafter, when thou art fallen.'—But he listened

---

[1] Query abhishekâdikâryata*h*?
[2] Cf. XIII, 3 and 14. Cf. also Lalitav. XXIV (arati?).

not to her words, closing his eyes in deep meditation like one who is sleepy.

17. Then Thirst, shameless like one distressed with thirst, thus addressed him who was free from all thirst: 'Fie, fie, thou hast abandoned thy family duties, thou hast fallen from all social obligations;

18. 'Without power no asceticism, sacrifice, or vow can be accomplished,—those great *Ri*shis Brahman and the rest, because they were endowed with power, enjoy their present triumph.

19. 'Know me to be the power called Thirst[1], and worship thirst accordingly; else I will clasp thee with all my might and fling away thy life.'

20. Motionless as one almost dead, he continued in meditation, remembering the former Buddhas; then Delight next tried to win him who was indeed hard to be won by evil deeds.

21. 'O holy one, I am Delight by name, fostering all practicable delights,—therefore making me the female mendicant's tutelary power, bring delight within thy reach.'

22. But whether flattered or threatened, whether she uttered curses or blessings, he remained absorbed in meditation, perfectly tranquil like one who has entered Nirvâ*n*a.

23. Then the three, with despondent faces, having retired together on one side, consulted with one another and came forward wearing the appearance of youthful beauty.

24. Folding their hands in reverence they thus addressed the Tathâgata, 'O holy one, receive us as religious mendicants, we are come to thy one refuge.

---

[1] Sc. Desire.

25. 'Having heard the fame of thy achievements, we, the daughters of Namuki, have come from the golden city, abandoning the life of a household.

26. 'We are desirous of repressing the teaching of our five hundred brothers,—we would be freed from a master, as thou thyself art freed from all passions.'

27. Having his mind continually guided by the conduct which leads to Nirvâna, and setting himself to remember the (former) Buddhas, he kept his eyes closed, absorbed in meditation.

28. Then again, having resolved on their new plan in concert, these enchantresses, assuming an older aspect, approached once more to delude him.

29. 'We have come here after wandering under the dismal avatâra of slaves[1],—thou art the avatâra of Buddha,—do thou establish us, mature, in the true Bauddha doctrine.

30. 'We are women of older age, much to be pitied, bewildered by the fear of death,—we are therefore worthy to be established in that doctrine of Nirvâna which puts an end to all future births.'

31. These words of the enchantresses were heard by him, yet he felt no anger; but they all became the victims of old age, through the manifestation of his divine power.

32. Having beheld him plunged in meditation, immovable like the mountain Meru,—they turned away their faces and they could not retain their beauty.

33. Bending their feet, with decrepit limbs, they

---

[1] I read dâsa- for dâsa-; could there be a reference to the ten avatâras?

thus addressed their father: 'O father, do thou, the lord of the world of Desire, restore us to our own forms.'

34. His daughters were dear, but he had no power to alter the effect of the will of Buddha; then their father said to them, 'Go to the refuge which he gives.'

35. Then they in various guises, bent humbly at his feet, implored the perfect Buddha, ' Pardon our transgression, whose minds were intoxicated with youth.'

36. The teacher, that mine of Forgiveness, in silence restored them by his will; and having repeatedly worshipped and praised him they went joyfully to their home.

37. Then again Mâra, the lord of the world of Desire, lost to shame, taking the form of the head of a family, thus addressed him from the sky:

38. 'I worshipped thee long ago, foretelling that thou wouldest become a Buddha; and by my blessings thou hast to-day become Buddha Tathâgata.

39. 'As thou didst come from thine own kingdom, so now having returned as Tathâgata, with a name corresponding to the reality be a king Tathâgata.

40. 'Having gone to that royal station, do thou meditate on the three jewels, and cherish thy father and mother, and delight Yasodharâ,—

41. 'Possessed of a thousand sons, and able to deliver the world, be successively the supreme lord of every world from the Yâma heaven onwards [1].

42. 'Having become also the supreme lord of all

---

[1] Mâra rules the four heavens from the Yâma to the Paranirmitavasavartin, Mahâbrahman the twenty Brahmalokas above them.

Bodhisattvas, thou shalt attain Nirvâna; O wise seer, repair to the hermitage of Kapila in order to beget those sons.

43. 'As thou art the king of the Law, so shall thy sons also be all Tathâgatas, and all the activity and cessation of existence shall depend upon thee, O Gina.'

44. To him thus speaking the All-wise replied, 'Hear, O shameless one; thou art Mâra, not the head of a clan, the upholder of the race of the Sâkyas.

45. 'A host like thee, though they came in myriads, could not harm me,—I will go to my kingdom gradually, I will bring the world to perfect happiness.

46. 'Thou art utterly vanquished, O Namuki, go back to thy own home; I will go hence to turn the wheel of the Law in Vârânasî.'

47. He, on hearing this command, saying with a deep sigh, 'Alas! I am crushed,' left him and went despondent and companionless through the sky to his home.

48. Then he, the conqueror of Mâra, rising from that throne, set forth to journey alone to the holy Vârânasî.

49. The heavens became covered with clouds when they saw the chief of saints, and the king of the Nâgas Mukilinda made a petition in reverential faith:

50. 'O holy one, thou art all-wise, there will be stormy weather for seven days,—wind, rain, and darkness,—dwell for the time in my abode.'

51. Though himself possessed of all supernatural power, the holy one thought of the world still involved in embodied existence, and sitting on that jewel-seat he remained absorbed in contemplation.

52. That king of the Nâgas there protected the Buddha, who is himself the source of all protection, from the rain, wind, and darkness, covering his body with his own hood.

53. When the seven days were past and the Nâga had paid his homage and was gone, the *G*ina proceeded to the bank of a river, near a forest of goat-herds[1].

54. As the Sugata stayed there during the night, a deity, who bore the name of the Indian fig-tree, came up to him, illumining the spot where he was, and thus addressed him with folded hands:

55. 'The fig-tree was planted by me when I was born as a man, bearing the name of Buddha; and it has been fostered like the Bodhi tree in the hope of delivering myself from evil.

56. 'By the merit of that action I myself have been born in heaven; in kindness to me, O my lord, do thou dwell seven days in triumph here.'

57. 'So be it,' said the chief of all saints, the true Kalpa tree to grant the wishes of the faithful votary, and he stayed under the fig-tree, absorbed in contemplation, spreading lustre around like a full moon.

58. There he dwelt seven days; and then in a forest of Datura trees, sitting at the foot of a palm, he remained absorbed in contemplation.

59. Spending thus in different spots his weeks of meditation, day and night, the great saint, pondering and fasting, went on in his way, longing to accomplish the world's salvation.

60. Then two wealthy merchants from the land

---

[1] A*g*apâlaka is in Pâli Costus speciosus; but it may here be a proper name.

of Uttara Utkala[1], named Trapusha and Bhallika, journeying with five hundred waggons,

61. Being freed from a sin which involved a birth as pretas[2], both joyfully worshipped Buddha with an offering of the three sweet substances[3] and milk; and they obtained thereby auspicious blessings.

62. They obtained pieces of his nails and hairs for a *K*aitya and they also received a prophecy of their future birth, and having received the additional promise, 'Ye shall also obtain a stone[4],' they then proceeded on their way elsewhere.

63. Then Buddha accepted alms in his bowl, offered by the goddess who dwelt in the Datura grove, and he blessed her with benedictions.

64. The *G*ina then blessed the four bowls as one, which were offered by the four Mahârâgas[5], and ate with pleasure the offering of milk.

65. Then one day the *G*ina ate there an Haritaki fruit[6] which was offered to him by *S*akra, and having planted the seed he caused it to grow to a tree.

66. The king of the Devas carried the news thereof joyfully to the Deva-heavens; and gods, men, and demons watered it with reverential circumambulations.

67. On hearing the news of the Haritaki seed, and remembering the whole history from first to last, a daughter of the gods named Bhadrikâ, who had been a cow in her former birth[7], came from heaven.

---

[1] Northern Orissa.
[2] Pretadosha? or the evil inflicted by a preta?
[3] Sc. sugar, honey, and ghee.
[4] With the mark of Buddha's feet on it?
[5] The rulers of the lowest devaloka.
[6] Terminalia chebula.   [7] Cf. Mahâbh. V, 7553.

68. She, the daughter of the gods, smiling with her companions, thus addressed the *G*ina, bringing him a garment of rags, dependent from a bough:

69. 'I beg to bring to thy notice—what? O Buddha!—accept this garment of rags, by whose influence I am now a daughter of heaven named Bhadrikâ.'

70. 'By the further development of this merit thou shalt become a Bodhisattva'—uttering this blessing the Teacher accepted the rags.

71. Beholding the tattered rags, the gods, crowding in the sky, filled with wonder, and uttering cries of hî hî, flung down upon him garments of heavenly silk.

72. 'These are not fit for a religious mendicant,' —so saying, he did not accept even one of them,— only thinking in his calm apathy, 'these are fit for imperial pomp and a householder's luxury.'

73. He desired a stone slab and some water in order to wash the dirt away,—*S*akra at that moment dug out a great river full of water;

74. And four stones are brought to him by the four Mahârâ*g*as,—on one he himself sat, on another he performed the washing;

75. On another he performed the drying, and another he flung up into the sky; the stone as it flew up reached the blazing city[1] and astonished all the worlds.

76. After paying their worship in many ways, Trapusha and Bhallika duly raised an excellent *K*aitya and they called it *S*ilâgarbha.

77. The ascetics of that neighbourhood paid their

---

[1] The sun? or the sphere of fire?

homage to the 'Three Stones' when they were made into a *K*aitya, and the noble stream flowed widely-known as the 'Holy River.'

78. Those who bathe and offer their worship in the holy river and reverence the *K*aitya of the three stones, become great-souled Bodhisattvas and obtain Nirvâ*n*a.

79. Then seated under a palm-tree the holy one pondered: 'The profound wisdom so hard to be understood is now known by me.

80. 'These sin-defiled worlds understand not this most excellent (Law), and the unenlightened shamelessly censure both me and my wisdom.

81. 'Shall I proclaim the Law? It is only produced by knowledge; having attained it thus in my lonely pondering, do I feel strong enough to deliver the world?'

82. Having remembered all that he had heard before, he again pondered; and resolving, 'I will explain it for the sake of delivering the world,'

83. Buddha, the chief of saints, absorbed in contemplation, shone forth, arousing[1] the world, having emitted in the darkness of the night a light from the tuft of hair between his eyebrows.

84. When it became dawn, Brahman and the other gods, and the various rulers of the different worlds, besought Sugata to turn the wheel of the Law.

85. When the *G*ina by his silence uttered an assenting 'so be it,' they returned to their own abodes; and the lion of the *S*âkyas also shone there, still remaining lost in contemplation.

86. Then the four divinities (of the Bodhi tree),

---

[1] Cf. sloka 118.

Dharmaruki and the rest, addressed him, 'Where, O teacher of the world, will the holy one turn the wheel of the Law?'

87. 'In Vârâṇasî, in the Deer Park will I turn the wheel of the Law; seated in the fourth posture[1], O deities, I will deliver the world.'

88. There the holy one, the bull of the Sâkya race, pondered, 'For whom shall I first turn the wheel of the Law?'

89. The glorious one reflected that [2] Rudraka and Arâḍa were dead[3], and then he remembered those others, the five men united in a worthy society[4], who dwelt at Kâsî.

90. Then Buddha set out to go joyfully to Kâsî, manifesting as he went the manifold supernatural course of life of Magadha.

91. Having made a mendicant (whom he met) happy in the path of those who are illustrious through the Law, the glorious one went on, illumining the country which lies to the north of Gayâ.

92. (Having stayed) in the dwelling of the prince of the Nâgas, named Sudarsana, on the occurrence of night, he ate a morning meal consisting of the five kinds of ambrosia, and departed, gladdening him with his blessing.

93. Near Vaṇârâ[5] he went under the shadow

---

[1] Sc. the padmâsana (Yoga-sûtras II, 46), described as that in which the left foot is bent between the right leg and thigh, and the right foot is bent between the left foot and thigh.

[2] It is written thus here, cf. XII, 86.   [3] Nirvâtau.

[4] Bhadravargîyâh, also called Pamkavargîyâh, cf. XII, 89.

[5] Query Varaṇâ, one of the rivers from which Benares is said to derive its name,—or is it a village near Vârâṇasî, the Anâla of the Lalitav. p. 528?

of a tree and there he established a poor Brâhman named Nandin in sacred knowledge.

94. In Vanârâ in a householder's dwelling he was lodged for the night; in the morning he partook of some milk and departed, having given his blessing.

95. In the village called Vumdadvîra he lodged in the abode of a Yaksha named Vumda[1], and in the morning after taking some milk and giving his blessing he departed.

96. Next was the garden named Rohitavastuka, and there the Nâga-king Kamandalu with his courtiers also worshipped him.

97. Having delivered various beings in every place, the compassionate saint journeyed on to Gandhapura and was worshipped there by the Yaksha Gandha.

98. When he arrived at the city Sârathi, the citizens volunteered to be charioteers in his service; thence he came to the Ganges, and he bade the ferryman cross.

99. 'Good man, convey me across the Ganges, may the seven blessings be thine.' 'I carry no one across unless he pays the fee.'

100. 'I have nothing, what shall I give?' So saying he went through the sky like the king of birds; and from that time Bimbisâra abolished the ferry-fee for all ascetics.

101. Then having entered Vârânasî, the Gina, illumining the city with his light, filled the minds of all the inhabitants of Kâsî with excessive interest.

---

[1] This may be Kumda.

102. In the Saṅkhamedhīya garden, the king of righteousness, absorbed in meditation, passed the night, gladdening like the moon all those who were astonished at his appearance.

103. The next day at the end of the second watch[1], having gone his begging round collecting alms, he, the unequalled one, like Hari, proceeded to the Deer Park.

104. The five disciples united in a worthy society[2], when they beheld him, said to one another, 'This is Gautama who has come hither, the ascetic who has abandoned his self-control.

105. 'He wanders about now, greedy[3], of impure soul, unstable and with his senses under no firm control, devoted to inquiries regarding the frying-pan.

106. 'We will not ask after his health, nor rise to meet him, nor address him, nor offer him a welcome, nor a seat, nor bid him enter into our dwelling.'

107. Having understood their agreement, with a smiling countenance, spreading light all around, Buddha advanced gradually nearer, holding his staff and his begging-pot.

108. Forgetful of their agreement, the five friends, under his constraining majesty, rose up like birds in their cages when scorched by fire.

109. Having taken his begging-bowl and staff, they gave him an arghya, and water for washing his feet and rinsing his mouth; and bowing

---

[1] Does this yâmadvaye mean at noon, counting the ahorâtra from sunrise to sunrise?

[2] Cf. supra, 89.   [3] Or perhaps 'irregular.'

reverentially they said to him, 'Honoured Sir, health to thee.'

110. 'Health in every respect is ours,—that wisdom has been attained which is so hard to be won,'—so saying, the holy one thus spoke to the five worthy associates:

111. 'But address me not as "worthy Sir,"— know that I am a *G*ina,—I have come to give the first wheel of the Law to you. Receive initiation from me,—ye shall obtain the place of Nirvâ*n*a.'

112. Then the five, pure in heart, begged leave to undertake his vow of a religious life; and the Buddha, touching their heads, received them into the mendicant order.

113. Then at the mendicants' respectful request the chief of saints bathed in the tank, and after eating ambrosia he reflected on the field of the Law[1].

114. Remembering that the Deer Park and the field of the *G*ina were there, he went joyfully with them and pointed out the sacred seats.

115. Having worshipped three seats, he desired to visit the fourth, and when the worthy disciples asked about it, the teacher thus addressed them:

116. 'These are the four seats of the Buddhas of the (present) Bhadra Age,—three Buddhas have passed therein, and I here am the fourth possessor of the ten powers.'

117. Having thus addressed them the glorious one bowed to that throne of the Law, decked with tapestries of cloth and silk, and having its stone

---

[1] Does this mean the country round Benares, as the land where all Buddhas turned the wheel of the Law?

inlaid with jewels, like a golden mountain, guarded by the kings of kings,

In the former fortnight of Âshâ*dh*a, on the day consecrated to the Regent of Jupiter, on the lunar day sacred to Vish*n*u, and on an auspicious conjunction, under the asterism Anurâdhâ[1], and in the muhûrta called the Victorious, in the night,—he took his stand on the throne.

118. The five worthy disciples stood in front, with joyful minds, paying their homage, and the son of *S*uddhodana performed that act of meditation which is called the Arouser of all worlds;

Brahman and the other gods came surrounded by their attendants, summoned each from his own world; and Maitrîya[2] with the deities of the Tushita heaven came for the turning of the wheel of the Law.

119. So too when the multitude of the sons of the *G*inas and the Suras gathered together from the ten directions of space, there came also the noble chief of the sons of the *G*inas, named Dharma-*k*akra[3], carrying the wheel of the Law;

With head reverentially bowed, having placed it, a mass of gold and jewels, before the Buddha and having worshipped him, he thus besought him, 'O thou lord of saints, turn the wheel of the Law as it has been done by (former) Sugatas.'

---

[1] The seventeenth Nakshatra.

[2] Is this the same as Maitreya, who is to be the future Buddha and who now awaits his time in the Tushita heaven? The Cambridge MS. interchanges Maitreya and Maitrîya in XVI, 53.

[3] 'Ein Buddha (der das Rad des Gesetzes in Bewegung setzt), Trikâ*nd*as. I, 1, 8.' St. Petersburg Dict.

BOOK XVI.

1. The omniscient lion of the Sâkyas then caused all the assembly, headed by those who belonged to the company of Maitrîya[1], to turn the wheel of the Law.

2. 'Listen, O company belonging to Maitrîya[1], ye who form one vast congregation,—as it was proclaimed by those past arch-saints, so is it now proclaimed by Me.

3. 'These are the two extremes, O mendicants, in the self-control of the religious ascetic,—the one which is devoted to the joys of desire, vulgar and common,

4. 'And the other which is tormented by the excessive pursuit of self-inflicted pain in the mortification of the soul's corruptions,—these are the two extremes of the religious ascetic, each devoted to that which is unworthy and useless.

5. 'These have nothing to do with true asceticism, renunciation of the world, or self-control, with true indifference or suppression of pain, or with any of the means of attaining deliverance.

6. 'They do not tend to the spiritual forms of knowledge, to wisdom, nor to Nirvâ*n*a; let him who is acquainted with the uselessness of inflicting pain and weariness on the body,

---

[1] The Maitrîya-vargiyâ*h*?

7. 'Who has lost his interest[1] in any pleasure or pain of a visible nature, or in the future, and who follows this middle Path for the good of the world,—

8. 'Let him, the Tathâgata, the teacher of the world, proclaim the good Law, beginning that manifestation of the good Law which consists of the (four) noble truths,

9. 'And let the Buddha proclaim the Path with its eight divisions. I too who am now the perfectly wise, and the Tathâgata in the world,

10. 'Will proclaim the noble Law, beginning with those sublime truths and the eightfold Path which is the means to attain perfect knowledge.

11. 'Instructing all the world I will show to it Nirvâna; those four noble truths must be heard first and comprehended by the soul.

12. 'That must be understood and thoroughly realised by the true students of wisdom, which has been known here by me, through the favour of all the Buddhas.

13. 'Having known the noble eightfold Path, and embraced it as realised with joy,—thus I declare to you the first means for the attainment of liberation.

14. 'Having thus commenced the noble truths, I will describe the true self-control; this noble truth is the best of all holy laws.

15. 'Walk as long as existence lasts, holding fast the noble eightfold Path,—this noble truth is the highest law for the attainment of true liberation.

16. 'Having pondered and held fast the noble

---

[1] Nirata seems used here for virata.

eightfold Path, walk in self-control; others, not understanding this, idle talkers full of self-conceit,

17. 'Say according to their own will that merit is the cause of corporeal existence, others maintain that the soul must be preserved (after death) for its merit is the cause of liberation.

18. 'Some say that everything comes spontaneously; others that the consequence was produced before; others talk loudly that all also depends on a Divine Lord.

19. 'If merit and demerit are produced by the good and evil fortune of the soul, how is it that good fortune does not always come to all embodied beings (at last), even in the absence of merit?

20. 'How is the difference accounted for, which we see in form, riches, happiness, and the rest,— if there are no previous actions, how do good and evil arise here?

21. 'If karman is said to be the cause of our actions, who would imagine cogency in this assumption? If all the world is produced spontaneously, who then would talk of the ownership of actions?

22. 'If good is caused by good, then evil will be the cause of evil,—how then could liberation from existence be produced by difficult penances[1]?

23. 'Others unwisely talk of Îsvara as a cause,— how then is there not uniformity in the world if Îsvara be the uniformly acting cause?

24. 'Thus certain ignorant people, talking loudly "he is," "he is not,"—through the demerits of their false theories, are at last born wretched in the different hells.

---

[1] I.e. viewed as an evil in themselves.

25. 'Through the merits of good theories virtuous men, who understand noble knowledge, go to heavenly worlds, from their self-restraint as regards body, speech, and thought.

26. 'All those who are devoted to existence are tormented with the swarms of its evils, and being consumed by old age, diseases, and death, each one dies and is born again.

27. 'There are many wise men here who can discourse on the laws of coming into being; but there is not even one who knows how the cessation of being is produced.

28. 'This body composed of the five skandhas, and produced from the five elements, is all empty and without soul, and arises from the action of the chain of causation.

29. 'This chain of causation is the cause of coming into existence, and the cessation of the series thereof is the cause of the state of cessation.

30. 'He who knowing this desires to promote the good of the world, let him hold fast the chain of causation, with his mind fixed on wisdom;

31. 'Let him embrace the vow of self-denial for the sake of wisdom, and practise the four perfections[1], and go through existence always doing good to all beings.

32. 'Then having become an Arhat and conquered all the wicked, even the hosts of Mâra, and attained the threefold wisdom, he shall enter Nirvâna.

33. 'Whosoever therefore has his mind indifferent

---

[1] The four brahmavihârâh, sc. charity, compassion, sympathy with others' joy, and stoicism.

and is void of all desire for any further form of existence, let him abolish one by one the several steps of the chain of causation[1].

34. 'When these effects of the chain of causation are thus one by one put an end to, he at last, being free from all stain and substratum, will pass into a blissful Nirvâ*n*a.

35. 'Listen all of you for your own happiness, with your minds free from stain,—I will declare to you step by step this chain of causation.

36. 'The idea of ignorance is what gives the root to the huge poison-tree of mundane existence with its trunk of pain.

37. 'The impressions[2] are caused by this, which produce [the acts of] the body, voice, and mind; and consciousness arises from these impressions, which produces as its development the five senses and the mind (or internal sense).

38. 'The organism[3] which is sometimes called sa*m*g*ñ*â or sa*m*darsana[4], springs from this; and from this arises the six organs of the senses, including mind.

39. 'The association of the six organs with their objects is called "contact;" and the consciousness of these different contacts is called "sensation[5];"

40. 'By this is produced thirst, which is the desire

---

[1] Cf. Childers in Colebrooke's Essays, I, p. 453.
[2] These sa*m*skârâ*h* constitute predispositions or tendencies.
[3] Literally 'the name and the form,' the individual, consisting of mind and body.
[4] The Nâmarûpa is properly the organised body (rûpa) and the three mental skandhas, vedanâ, sa*m*g*ñ*â, and the sa*m*skârâ*h*, which are together called nâma.
[5] Vedanâ.

of being troubled[1] by worldly objects; "attachment to continued existence," arising from this, sets itself in action towards pleasure and the rest;

41. 'From attachment springs continued existence, which is sensual, possessing form, or formless[2]; and from existence arises birth through a returning to various wombs.

42. 'On birth is dependent the series of old age, death, sorrow and the like; by putting a stop to ignorance and what follows from it, all these successively surcease.

43. 'This is the chain of causation, having many turns, and whose sphere of action is created by ignorance,—this is to be meditated upon by you who enjoy the calm of dwelling tranquilly in lonely woods[3];

'He who knows it thoroughly reaches at last to absolute tenuity; and having become thus attenuated he becomes blissfully extinct.

44. 'When you have thus learned this, in order to be freed from the bond of existence, you must cut down with all your efforts the root of pain, ignorance.

45. 'Then, being set free from the bonds of the prison-house of existence, as Arhats, possessing natures perfectly pure, you shall attain Nirvâ*n*a.'

46. Having heard this lesson preached by the chief of saints, all the mendicants comprehended the course and the cessation of embodied existence.

---

[1] Sa*m*kle*s*a,—should we read sa*ms*lesha?

[2] I.e. in the eleven kâmalokas, the sixteen rûpabrahmalokas, and the four arûpabrahmalokas.

[3] The metre shows that two short syllables are wanting in the line, vi*g*ana (vana) vi*s*râma*s*amibhi*h*.

47. As these five ascetics listened to his words, their intellectual eye was purified for the attainment of perfect wisdom:

48. The eye of dharma[1] was purified in six hundred millions of gods, and the eye of wisdom in eight hundred millions of Brahmans[2].

49. The eye of dharma was purified in eighty thousand men, and even in all beings an ardour for the Law was made visible.

50. Everywhere all kinds of evil became tranquillised, and on every side an ardour for all that helps on the good Law manifested itself.

51. In the heavens everywhere the heavenly beings with troops of Apsarases uttered forth great shouts, 'Even so, O noble being of boundless energy!'

52. Then Maitreya addressed the holy one, 'O great mendicant, in what form has the wheel been turned by thee?'

53. Having heard this question asked by the great-souled Maitreya, the holy one looked at him and thus addressed him:

54. 'The profound subtil wheel of the Law, so hard to be seen, has been turned by me, into which the disputatious Tîrthikas cannot penetrate.

55. 'The wheel of the Law has been turned, which has no extension, no origin, no birth, no home, isolated, and free from matter;

56. 'Having many divisions, and not being without divisions[3], having no cause, and susceptible of no definition,—that wheel, which is described as

---

[1] Dharmakakshuḥ, the eye to discern the Law?
[2] The divine inhabitants of the Brahmalokas.
[3] Anirvyûham?

possessing perfect equilibrium, has been proclaimed by the Buddha.

57. 'Everything subject to successive causation is like a delusion, a mirage, or a dream, like the moon seen in water or an echo,—it lies stretched out on the surface, not to be extirpated, but not eternal.

58. ' The wheel of the Law has been described as that in which all false doctrines are extirpated; it is always like the pure ether, involving no doubts, ever bright.

59. ' The wheel of the Law is described as without end or middle, existing apart from " it is " or " it is not," separated from soul or soullessness.

60. ' The wheel of the Law has been here set forth, with a description according to its real nature, —as it has a limit and as it has not a limit, in its actual quantity and quality.

61. ' The wheel of the Law has been here set forth, described as possessing unique attributes, apart from the power of the eye and so too as regards the sense of hearing or smell;

62. 'Apart from the tongue, the touch, or the mind,—without soul or exertion ;

' Such is this wheel of the Law which has been turned by me;

63. ' He makes wise all the ignorant,—therefore is he called the Buddha [1]; this knowledge of the laws of reality has been ascertained by me of myself,

64. ' Apart from all teaching by another, therefore is he called the self-existent,—having all laws under his control, therefore is he called the lord of Law.

65. ' He knows what is right (naya) and wrong (anaya) in laws, therefore is he called Nâyaka; he

---

[1] Buddha seems here to identify himself with his Law.

teaches unnumbered beings as they become fit to be taught.

66. 'He has reached the furthest limit of instruction, therefore is he called Vinâyaka, from his pointing out the best of good paths to beings who have lost their way.

67. 'He has reached the furthest limit of good teaching, he is the guide to all the Law,—attracting all beings by his knowledge of all the means of conciliation;

68. 'He has passed through the forest of mundane existence, therefore is he called the Leader of the Caravan; the absolute ruler over all law, therefore he is the *Gi*na, the lord of Law.

69. 'From his turning the wheel of the Law he is the lord of all the sovereigns of Law; the master-giver of the Law, the teacher, the master of the Law, the lord of the world;

70. 'He who has offered the sacrifice, accomplished his end, fulfilled his hope, achieved his success, the consoler, the loving regarder, the hero, the champion, the victorious one in conflict;

71. 'He has come out from all conflict, released himself and the releaser of all,—he is become the light of the world, the illuminator of the knowledge of true wisdom;

72. 'The dispeller of the darkness of ignorance, the illuminer of the great torch, the great physician, the great seer, the healer of all evils,

73. 'The extractor of the barb of evil from all those who are wounded by evil,—he who is possessed of all distinctive marks and adorned with all signs,

74. 'With his body and limbs every way perfect,

of pure conduct and perfectly clear mind, possessed of the ten powers, having great fortitude, learned with all learning,

75. 'Endowed with all the independent states [1], he who has attained the great Yâna, the lord of all Dharma, the ruler, the monarch of all worlds, the sovereign,

76. 'The lord of all wisdom, the wise, the destroyer of the pride of all disputers, the omniscient, the Arhat, possessed of the perfect knowledge, the great Buddha, the lord of saints;

77. 'The victorious triumphant overthrower of the insolence and pride of the evil Mâra, the perfect Buddha, the Sugata, the wise one, he who brings the desired end to all beings,

78. 'Ever cognisant of past acts, never speaking falsely, a mine of perfect excellence and of all good qualities, the destroyer of all evil ways, the guide in all good ways [2],

79. 'The ruler of the world, the bearer of the world, the master of the world, the sovereign of the world, the teacher of the world, the preceptor of the world, he who brings to the world the Law, virtue, and its true end,

80. 'The fount of an ambrosia which quenches the scorching of the flame of all pain, and the powerful luminary which dries up the great ocean of all pain,

81. 'He who brings all virtue and all true wealth, the possessor of perfect excellence and all good qualities, the guide on the road of wisdom, he who shows the way to Nirvâ*n*a,

---

[1] Eighteen in all. See Burnouf, Lotus, pp. 648, &c.
[2] Query sadv*r*itti for sa*m*v*r*itti?

82. 'The Tathâgata, without stain, without attachment, without uncertainty.—This is the compendious declaration in the turning of the wheel of the Law.

83. 'A concise manifestation of a Tathâgata's qualities is now declared by me; for a Buddha's knowledge is endless, unlimited like the ether;

84. 'A narrator might spend a Kalpa, but the virtues of the Buddha would not come to an end,—thus by me has the multitude of the virtues of the Buddha been described.

85. 'Having heard this and welcomed it with joy go on ever in happiness; this, Sirs, is the Mahâyâna, the instrument of the Law of the perfect Buddha, which is the establisher of the welfare of all beings, set forth by all the Buddhas.

86. 'In order that this methodical arrangement of the Law may be always spread abroad, do you yourselves always proclaim it and hand it on.

87. 'Whosoever, Sirs, hears, sees, and welcomes with joy this methodical arrangement of the Law, which is a mine of happiness and prosperity, and honours it with folded hands,

88. 'Shall attain pre-eminent strength with a glorious form and limbs, and a retinue of the holy, and an intelligence of the highest reach,

89. 'And the happiness of perfect contemplation, with a deep calm[1] of uninterrupted bliss, with his senses in their highest perfection, and illuminated by unclouded knowledge.

90. 'He shall assuredly attain these eight pre-eminent perfections, who hears and sees this Law

---

[1] I read naishkarmya for naishkramya.

with a serene soul and worships it with folded hands.

91. 'Whosoever in the midst of the assembly shall gladly offer a pulpit to the high-minded teacher of the great Law,

92. 'That virtuous man shall assuredly attain the seat of the most excellent, and also the seat of a householder, and the throne of a universal monarch;

93. 'He shall also attain the throne of one of the guardian-spirits of the world, and also the firm throne of *S*akra, and also the throne of the Va*s*avartina*h* gods, aye, and the supreme throne of Brahman;

94. 'And also with the permission of the Bodhisattva who is seated on the Bodhi throne he shall obtain the throne of a teacher of the good Law who has risen to perfect knowledge.

95. 'These eight seats shall the pure-souled one attain who offers joyfully a seat to him who proclaims the Law.

96. 'Whosoever with a believing heart, after examination, shall utter applause to the pious man who proclaims this carefully arranged Law;

97. 'Shall become a truthful and pure speaker, and one whose words are to be accepted,—one whose utterances are welcome and delightful, whose voice is sweet and gentle;

98. 'Having a voice like a Kalavi*n*ka bird [1], with a deep and sweet tone, having also a pure voice like Brahman's [2], and a loud voice with a lion's sound.

99. 'He as an all-wise and truthful speaker shall

---

[1] A kind of sparrow.
[2] Or 'having a voice of pure spiritual truth?'

obtain these eight excellences of speech, who utters applause to one who proclaims the good Law.

100. 'And whosoever, after writing this method of the Law in a book, shall set it in his house and always worship it and honour it with all reverential observances,

101. 'And uttering its praises shall hand the doctrine onward on every side, he, the very pious man, shall obtain a most excellent treasure of memory,

102. 'And a treasure of insight[1], and a treasure of prudence[2], and a treasure of good spells, and a treasure full of intelligence,

103. 'And a treasure of the highest wisdom, and the most excellent treasure of the Law, and a treasure of knowledge, the means to attain the excellences of the good Law,—

104. 'These eight treasures shall that high-minded man attain who joyfully writes this down and sets it in a sure place and always worships it.

105. 'And he who, himself holding this method of the Law in his mind, sets it going around him, shall obtain a complete supply for liberality for the good of the world, .

106. 'Next, a complete supply of virtuous dispositions, a most excellent supply of sacred knowledge, a supply of perfect calmness, and that which is called spiritual insight,

107. 'A supply of the merit caused by the good Law, a most excellent supply of knowledge, a supply of boundless compassion, which is the means to attain the virtues of the perfect Buddha.

---

[1] I read mahâmatinidhânam for mahâprati-.
[2] Gati? 'resources?'

108. 'He, full of joy, shall obtain these eight supplies who himself holds this method of the Law in his mind and sets it going abroad.

109. 'And he who shall declare this method of the Law to others, shall have himself purified by great merit and shall be prosperous and possessed of supernatural powers.

110. 'He shall become a universal monarch, a king of kings, and even a ruler among the guardians of the world [1], an Indra ruler of the gods [2], and even the ruler of the Yâma heaven [3],

111. 'Yea, the ruler of the Tushita heaven, and the ruler of the Sunirmitâ*h*, and the king of the Va*s*avartina*h* [4], and the lord of the Brahmaloka;

112. 'Yea, Mahâbrahman, the highest of Sages,— and in the end he shall even become a Buddha,—he, possessing a thoroughly pure intelligence, shall obtain these eight sublime rewards of merit.

113. 'And he who, thoroughly intent, with a believing heart, and filled with faith and devotion, shall hear this method of the Law as it is preached,

114. 'He shall have his intellect made perfectly pure, his mind calmed with boundless charity, and his soul happy with boundless compassion, and he shall be filled with boundless joy;

115. 'His soul constantly calm with universal indifference, rejoicing in the four contemplations, having reached the ecstatic state of absolute indifference [5], and with his senses abolished,

116. 'With the five transcendent faculties attained,

---

[1] Sc. the Mahârâ*g*as of the first heaven.
[2] In the second Devaloka.   [3] The third Devaloka.
[4] These are the fourth, fifth, and sixth Devalokas.
[5] Samârûpya?

and destroying the aggregate of latent impressions, he, endowed with supernatural powers, will attain the samâdhi called *Sûra*m*gama.*

117. 'He, having his soul pure, will attain these eight forms of absolute spotlessness; yea, wherever this method of the Law will prevail universally,

118. 'There will be no fear of any disturbance in the kingdom, no fear of evil-minded thieves, nor fear of evil beasts;

119. 'There will be no fear of plagues, famines, or wildernesses; and no alarm shall spread, caused by quarrel or war;

120. 'There shall be no fear from the gods nor from Nâgas, Yakshas, and the like, nor shall there be anywhere any fear of any misfortune.

121. 'These eight fears shall not be found there where this Law extends; it is all briefly explained, my friends,—all that arises from holding it stedfastly.

122. 'A yet higher and most excellent merit is declared by all the Buddhas, even although all living beings were to practise complete self-restraint.

123. 'Let a man worship the Buddhas, honouring them always with faith; from that comes this pre-eminent merit, as is declared by the *G*inas.

124. 'And whosoever joyfully worships a Pratyeka-Buddha, they shall become themselves Pratyeka-Buddhas; therefore let every one worship them.

125. 'There is pre-eminent merit from the worship of one Bodhisattva, and they shall all themselves become Bodhisattvas, let every one worship them;

126. 'Therefore there is pre-eminent merit from the worship of one Buddha,—they shall all them-

selves become *G*inas, let every one devoutly worship them; and he too shall obtain this pre-eminent merit who hears this or causes others to hear it.

127. 'And whosoever in days when the good Law is abolished abandons love for his own body and life and proclaims day and night these good words, —pre-eminent is his merit from this.

128. 'He who wishes to worship constantly the lords of saints, the Pratyeka-Buddhas and the Arhats, let him resolutely produce in his mind the idea of true wisdom and proclaim these good words and the Law.

129. 'This jewel of all good doctrines, which is uttered by the Buddhas for the good of all beings, —even one who lives in a house will be a Tathâgata for it, where this good doctrine prevails.

130. 'He obtains a glorious and endless splendour who teaches even one word thereof; he will not miss one consonant nor the meaning who gives this Sûtra to others.

131. 'He is the best of all guides of men, no other being is like unto him; he is like a jewel, of imperishable glory, who hears this Law with a pure heart.

132. 'Therefore let those who are endowed with lofty ambitions, always hear this Law which causes transcendent merit; let them hear it and gladly welcome it and lay it up in their minds and continually worship the three jewels with faith.'

BOOK XVII.

[1 [1]. When the heavenly beings with Brahman at their head and the Bodhisattvas intent on self-mortification[2] heard this glorification of the Law uttered by the lion of the *S*âkyas, they were desirous to hear again this which is so difficult to find, and they went to the city and worshipped him, propitiating his favour; in the dark fortnight of the month Âsha*dh*a on the lunar day sacred to Agni, with the moon in the constellation called Kar*n*a (?) and on an auspicious day,—he, remembering the Buddha worlds and being desirous to save all creatures, set off on his journey, longing for disciples with his father at their head.]

2. The associated Brâhmans, accompanied by the inhabitants of Kâ*s*î who had gone to the Deer Park, and the mendicants to the number of thirty, were rendered resplendent by the chief of saints; Kâsikâ the harlot of Kâ*s*î went to the heaven of the gods, after she had worshipped the *G*ina and attached her sons to the service of the glorious one; the conqueror of the world then made thirty rejoicing officiating priests of Kâ*s*î his disciples, initiating them in the course of perfect wisdom; and the son of Maitrâya*n*î[3] and Maitra, the preceptor of hosts of the twice-born, named Pûr*n*a, obtained true wisdom from the chief of saints and became a noble mendicant.

3. The priest of the lord of the city Marakata, a

---

[1] This is a doubtful verse, the metre is faulty.
[2] I read tapasyâpare.   [3] Burnouf, Lotus, p. 489.

Brâhman named A*g*aya, and his son Nâlaka, well versed in sacred learning and full of answers to questions, and an ascetic named Dh*r*iti, dwelling in the Vindhya, and an invincible Brâhman ascetic Sa*m*gayin with his disciples,—these all, dwellers in the Vindhya,—when they came to him for refuge, the chief of saints initiated as mendicants, touching them with his hand bearing the mark of a wheel; moreover the Nâga Elapatra came to the abode of the best of saints, and stood resplendent there, perfectly calm in his demeanour and worshipping him with his rosaries.

4. There was also a female ascetic of Mathurâ named Trikavya*m*gikâ, and a Brâhman named Vidyâkara,—their son was named Sabhya, a dweller in the district called *S*vetabâlârka, a wise ascetic, proud of his wisdom,—he went into the Deer Park, wearing the aspect of one perfectly illumined, and desiring the highest wisdom from the chief of mendicants; seeking from the omniscient admission to the noble life, he became renowned as the mendicant Sabhya in all assemblies.

5. The son of Lalitâprabudhâ, born after worship paid to the best of trees on the bank of the stream Vara*n*â,—renowned in the world as Ya*s*oda,—wise from the besprinkling of the ambrosia of the words of the king of heaven,—remembering all former discourses which he had heard, came with his friends to the wood in the Deer Park, accompanied by his glory; and the holy one, touching his head with his hand, made him the guru of the chief Bhikshus.

6. The glorious one, named the great Buddha, proceeded with the mendicants in an auspicious company, and having manifested his triumphal march for the salvation of the world, entered the city of Kâ*s*i.

A poor Brâhman, named Svastika, a native of Vârâ*n*asî, obtained riches from heaven through the favour of the glorious one, and having received adoption as a slave in the *G*ina faith, became a mendicant and an Arhat at the hands of the great teacher.

7. Blessing the king of Kâ*si*[1] Divodâsa and the citizens with gold, corn, and other riches,—taking up his abode in different places in forests, caves, mountains, he at last came in his rambles to the river *G*âhnavî. The boatman who conveyed the *G*ina across the Ganges worshipped him and offered him milk with due services of reverence, and became a mendicant through his favour and by the *G*ina's command found a dwelling in the Buddha's hermitage in the grove.

8. The glorious one, after he had crossed the Ganges, went to the hermitage of Kâsyapa at Gayâ, called Uruvilva; there, having shown his supernatural power, he received as Bhikshus the Kâ*s*yapas, Uruvilva, and others, with more than a thousand of their disciples, having endued them forthwith with all kinds of spiritual knowledge and with the power to abandon all worldly action; then accompanied by three hundred disciples Upasena at the command of his maternal uncle became an ascetic.

9. The glorious one made seven hundred ascetics enter Nirvâ*n*a who dwelt in the wood Dharma; and the lord of the Law also caused the daughters of Na*m*dika, Su*g*âtâ and others, who dwelt in the village, to become the first female ascetics; and in the city of Râ*g*ag*ri*ha, having enlightened in right action and in activity the king Bimbisâra,

---

[1] Kâ*s*ikâ.

the monarch, who is to be considered as the elder-born in perfect knowledge, he made him who was the devoted follower of the Buddha, a Bodhisattva and a Sak*ri*dâgâmin.

10. In another village named Nâradya there was a Brâhman Dharmapâlin and a Brâhman woman named *S*âlyâ; their seventh son named Upatishya [1], who had studied the entire Veda, became a Buddhist mendicant; so too there was a great pa*nd*it, a Brâhman named Dhânyâyana, who dwelt in the village Kolata, and his son;—him and the son of *S*âli named Maudgalya the great saint received as the best of Bhikshus, pre-eminent disciples.

11. Next he ordained as a mendicant the keen-witted maternal uncle of *S*âliputra [1], Dirghânakha by name; then travelling in the realm of Magadha, the glorious one, being honoured by the inhabitants with alms and other signs of devotion, and delivering them from evil, dwelt in the convent given by the seer *G*eta, attracting to himself many of the monks; and after ordaining as a mendicant a native of Mithilâ, named Ânanda, with his companions, he dwelt there a year.

12. The Brâhman named Kâ*s*yapa, a very Kuvera for wealth, and a master in all the sciences connected with the Veda, an inhabitant of Râ*g*ageha, being pure-minded and wearing only one garment, left all his kindred and came seeking wisdom in asceticism; —when this noble youth came to the Bodhi tree and practised for six years a penance hard to carry out, then he paid worship to the chief of saints who had attained perfect knowledge, and he became the well-

---

[1] Sc. *S*âriputra.

known Kâsyapa, the chief of ascetics, the foremost of the Arhats.

13. The saint Naradatta, dwelling on Mount Himavat, remembering the wholesome words of his maternal uncle, came to the Sugata with his disciples, and the holy one admitted them all into the order of the Gina; then a woman named Sakti, and another named Kamalâ, pre-eminent in Brâhmanical power, came to the Sugata and fell down at his feet, and then standing before him they were received by the saint, and made happy with the staff and begging-bowl.

14. Seven hundred disciples of the ascetic Rudraka, remembering the noble words of their teacher, becoming mendicants according to the doctrine of the Gina, flocked round him paying him their homage and carrying their staves; next a seer, named Raivata, joyfully uttering his praises, having finished his course of discipline, became a mendicant, full of devotion to the guru, counting gold and clay as the same, well versed in sacred spells and meditation, and able to counteract the three kinds of poisons and other fatal harms.

15. Having received as followers and disciples certain householders of Srâvastî, Pûrna and others, and given them alms-vessels,—and having made many poor wretches as rich as Kuvera, and maimed persons with all their limbs perfect, and paupers and orphans affluent,—and having proclaimed the Law, and dwelt two years in the forest Getaka delivering the suppliants, the glorious one, having taught again the saint Geta, and established the Bhikshu Pûrna, once more proceeded on his way.

16. Then the glorious one went on, protecting

the merchant-caravans by the stores of his own treasures from the troops of robbers, next he went into the neighbourhood of Râ*g*ageha wandering with his begging-vessel which had been given by the merchants. In the wood called Ve*n*u, filled with *S*âl trees, he ate an offering of food prepared by the enriched robbers, and he received as mendicants five hundred of them and gave them their begging-vessels and the other requisites.

17. At the invitation of Buddha's son, *S*uddhodana gave this message to his envoys *Kh*andaka and Udâyin, 'Thy father and mother, some noble ladies, headed by Ya*s*odr*i*h, and this my young son have come in the hope of seeing thee, under the idea that thou art devoted to the world's salvation; what shall I tell them?' They two went, and reverentially saluting the Buddha in the vihâra called Ve*n*u, they told him the message with their eyes filled with tears.

18. *Kh*andaka and Udâyin accepted his counsel, and, being delighted at the mighty power of Buddha, became great ascetics; and the great *G*ina took them with him and proceeded from that wood with the disciples, the mendicants, and the saints. Going on from place to place, and dwelling in each for a while and conferring deliverance and confirming the disciples, the mendicants, and the Arhats, he at last reached the wood Nigrodha, illuminating the district by his glory, shaking the earth and putting an end to misery.

19. [1] He again stirred up his followers in the doctrine of the Buddha, and then went on with the

---

[1] Several phrases are obscure in this verse.

crowds of inhabitants gathered round him, instructing his shaven mendicant-followers, as they begged alms, while the gods brought his precepts to their minds[1]. He forbade the mendicants to enter the city and went to Râgageha himself with his own followers; and then the king who dwells apart from all doubt[2], the *G*ina, who knows at once all the history of every Bhikshu, instructed the ascetic (Udâyin) in proclaiming wisdom to others.

20. In accordance with the *G*ina's command that prince of ascetics, Udâyin, went to the city of Kapila; there he, the lord of all possessors of supernatural powers, instructed the king as he stood in the assembly in the boon of the eight hundred powers; and coming down from heaven he uttered to the king and his court a discourse on the four sublime truths, and the king, with his mind enlightened, having worshipped him, held intercourse with him, attended by his courtiers, offering every form of homage.

21. The monarch, rejoiced at the sight of the *G*ina, praised his feet, worshipping them with eight hundred presents; and the Sugata departed, and made manifest in the sky in his one person a form comprehending the universe; first as fire, then ambrosia, then the king of beasts, an elephant, the king of horses, the king of peacocks[3], the king of birds, Maghavan, the ten rulers of the world headed by Yama, the sun, the moon, the hosts of stars, Brahman, Vish*n*u, and *S*iva.

22. The sons of Diti, the four (Mahârâgas) with

---

[1] Obscure. [2] Dvâpare‧stha?
[3] *S*ikhirâ*t* might mean 'the king of flames,' &c.

Dhritarâshtra at their head, the hosts of Yogins with the king Drumasiddha, the (heavenly) ascetics, the Vasus, the Manus, the sons of the forest, the creatures of the waters headed by the makara, the birds headed by Garuda, and all the kings in the different worlds with the lord of the Tushita heaven at their head, and those in the world of the dead[1] the domain of Bali,—whatever is conspicuous in the universe the holy one created it all, becoming the universal one.

23. When the king had thus been instructed, the lord of saints went to the Satya heaven, and then from the sky, seated on his own throne[2], he proclaimed the twelvefold Law; then he restored Gautamî and Anugopâ and many other women to sight, and filled all the assembled people with joy; and established others in Nirvâna and in the Law. Then Suddhodana full of joy invited him to a feast given to the whole assembly, and he accepted it by his silence.

24. The lion of the Sâkyas, having been thus invited, went with the congregation of his followers to the place, after having shown a mighty miracle. Then the earth shook, a shower of flowers fell, the various quarters of space became illumined and a wind blew; and the heavenly beings, Brahman, Siva, Vishnu, Indra, Yama, Varuna, Kuvera, the lord of Bhûtas, the lord of the winds, Nirriti, Fire with his seven flames, and the rest, stood resting their feet on the serpent Sesha, and followed leading the gods and gandharvas in their dance in the sky.

25. Making millions of ascetics, disciples, Arhats,

---

[1] Martya seems here to be used for mrita.
[2] Or must we take sva as put for svar, 'in heaven?'

sages, mendicants, and fasters,—and delivering from their ills the blind, the humpbacked, the lame, the insane, the maimed as well as the destitute,—and having established many persons of the fourth caste in the true activity and inaction and in the three yânas[1], with the four sa*m*grahas[2] and the eight a*m*gas[3],—going on from place to place, delivering, and confirming the Bhikshus, in the twelfth year he went to his own city.

26. Day by day confirming the Bhikshus, and providing food for the congregation, in an auspicious moment he made a journey to Lumbinî with the Bhikshus and the citizens, Brahman and Rudra being at their head, with great triumph and noise of musical instruments. There he saw the holy fig-tree and he stood by it remembering his birth, with a smile; and rays of light streamed from his mouth and went forth illumining the earth; and he uttered a discourse to the goddess of the wood, giving her the serenity of faith.

27. 'Having come to the Lumbinî fig-tree he spoke to Paurvikâ the daughter of Râhula, and Gopikâ the daughter of Maitra, and his own Saudhanî Kausikâ; and he uttered an affectionate discourse honouring his mother by the tank Vasatya; then speaking with Eka*s*a*m*gî the daughter of Mahâ-kautuka and Sautasomî in the wood Nigrodha, he received into the community some members of his own family, headed by Sundarânanda, and one hundred and seven citizens.

---

[1] Burnouf, Lotus, p. 315.
[2] Apparently the four means of conciliating dependents.
[3] The eightfold path of Buddhist morality.
[4] Much of this stanza is obscure.

28. Having declared the glory of the Law of Buddha, he built a round Stûpa and gave a royal coronation to Saunu¹, sending him into the wood pre-eminent with the holiest saints and *K*aityas, and bidding him worship the sacred relics; and having commanded Râhula, Gautamî, and the other women led by Gopikâ, with staves in their hands, as shaven ascetics, to practise the vow of fasting called ahoratra², and after that the Laksha*k*aitya ceremony³ and then the rite called *Sri*ṅgabheri⁴, and that called Vasu*m*dhârikâ⁵.

29. The Ash*t*asâhasrikâ of sacred authority⁶,— the Geya⁷ and the Gâthâ, the Nidâna and the Avadâna, and that which is called the Sûtra of the great Yâna, the Vyâkara⁸ and the Ityukta, the *G*âtaka, the work called Vaipulya, the Adbhuta⁹ and the Upade*s*a, and also the Udânaka¹⁰ as the twelfth.—Teaching (these sacred texts) and making current the Yâna for common disciples, that for Pratyeka Buddhas, and the Mahâyâna, and proclaiming them all around, accompanied by thirteen and a half bodies of mendicants, the conqueror of the world went out of the city of Kapila.

30. After displaying miracles in the city of Ka-

---

¹ Or the grandson of the king?
² See Râ*g*endralâl Mitra, Nepalese Buddhist Literature, p. 221.
³ Ibid. p. 275.   ⁴ Ibid. p. 230.   ⁵ Ibid. p. 271.
⁶ Naigamâ? The Ash*t*asâhasrikâ seems not to be reckoned here among the following twelve texts of peculiar authority with the Northern Buddhists. But Burnouf's authorities include it in that called 'Sûtra.'
⁷ For the following twelve names see Burnouf, Introd. pp. 51–66.
⁸ More properly Vyâkara*n*a.
⁹ Burnouf calls it adbhutadharma.
¹⁰ Burnouf, Introd. p. 58.

pila, and having paid honour to his father, and having made Râhula and his companions Arhats, and also the Bhikshu*n*is with Gautamî and Gopikâ at their head, and various women of all the four castes; and having established Saunu[1] on his imperial throne, and the people in the *G*ina doctrine, and having abolished poverty and darkness, and then remembering his mother, he set forth, after worshipping Svaya*m*bhû, towards the northern region with Brahman, Vish*n*u, and *S*iva as mendicants in his train.

31. The glory of the Avadâna of the birth of the lion of the *S*âkyas has thus been described by me at length and yet very concisely; it must be corrected by pa*nd*its wherever anything is omitted,—my childish speech is not to be laughed at, but to be listened to with pleasure.

Whatever virtue I may have acquired from describing the king of the Law, the deliverer from mundane existence, who assumes all forms,—may it become a store of merit for the production of right activity and inactivity in others, and for the diffusion of delight among the six orders of beings[2].

Thus ends the seventeenth sarga, called the Progress to Lumbinî, in the great poem made by A*s*vaghosha, the Buddha-*k*arita[3].

---

[1] Or Saunava, see *s*loka 28.

[2] Sc. the sha*d g*atayas, the 'six paths,' are gods, men, Asuras, &c., Pretas, brutes, and the inhabitants of the different hells.

[3] C adds here on the last page the following lines: 'The poem about Buddha, very difficult to obtain, was written by Am*ri*ânanda in the year indicated by a cipher, the arrows (of Kâma), and a nine [=Newâr Sa*m*vat 950, or A.D. 1830], in the dark fortnight of the month Mârga*s*irsha (Nov.–Dec.) and on the day ruled by the

seventh astrological house Smara. Having searched for them everywhere and not found them, four sargas have been made by me,—the fourteenth, fifteenth, sixteenth, and seventeenth.' The beginning of another version of these lines is given in P, but D omits them. The name of Amrïtânanda occurs in Râgendralâl Mitra's Nepalese Buddhist Literature as the author of three treatises,—two in Sanskrit, the *Khando*mrïtalatâ* (p. 79), the Kalyânapamkavimsatikâ (p. 99), translated in Wilson's Works, vol. ii, and the Vîrakusâvadâna (p. 274) in Newârî. Compare Cowell and Eggeling's Catalogue, pp. 18, 24; in p. 18 he is associated with the date N.S. 916 (A.D. 1796).

INDEX OF PROPER NAMES[1].

Akanish*th*â*h*, the, book V, verse 47.
Akshamâlâ, IV, 77.
Agastya, IV, 73; IX, 9, 26.
Agni, IV, 76; VII, 17.
Agni, son of, (Skanda), I, 66.
A*m*giras, I, 46; IX, 10.
A*m*girasas, the, II, 36.
Aga, VIII, 79.
Agapâla-vana, XV, 53.
Agaya, XVII, 3.
Atri, I, 48.
Anugopâ, XVII, 23.
A*m*tideva, I, 57; IX, 20, 60.
A*m*dhakas, the, XI, 31.
Apsaras, I, 94; IV, 11, 28, &c.
A*m*barîsha, IX, 59.
Arâ*d*a, VII, 54; IX, 6; XI, 69; XII, 1-81; XV, 89.
Alakâ, III, 65.
A*s*vinau, the, VII, 7.
Asita, I, 54, 67, 85; II, 25; VIII, 84.
Ahalyâ, IV, 72.

Âki*m*kanyâ*h*, XII, 63 (cf. 83).
Âtreya, I, 48.
Ânanda, XVII, 11.
Âbhasurâ*h*, the, XII, 53.
Âshâ*dh*a, IX, 20.

Ikshvâkavas, the, I, 49; VII, 6; IX, 4; XII, 1.
Indra (Maghavat, *S*akra, &c.), I, 7, 27, 29, 63, 92; II, 27; IV, 72; V, 22, 27, 87; VI, 62; VII, 3, 43; VIII, 13, 64, 73, 79; IX, 5, 10, 12; X, 19, 39, 41; XI, 13, 14, 16, 70; XIII, 9, 37; XV, 65, 73; XVI, 93, 110.

Î*s*vara, Î*s*a, IX, 53; X, 3; XVII, 21, 24, 30.

Ugrâyudha, XI, 18.
Uttare kurava*h*, the, IV, 10.
Udâyin, IV, 8, 24, 62; XVII, 17, 18, 20.
Udraka, XII, 82-86 (cf. Rudraka).
Upatishya, XVII, 10.
Upasu*m*da, XI, 32.
Upasena, XVII, 8.
Uruvilva, XVII, 8.
Urva*s*î, XI, 15.

Rishya*s*ri*m*ga, IV, 19.

Eka*s*a*m*gî, XVII, 27.
Elapatra, XVII, 3.

Ai*d*a, XI, 15; XIII, 12.

Autathya, IV, 74.
Aurva, I, 29.
Aurva*s*eya, IX, 9.

Ka, II, 51; XI, 61 (?).
Kakshîvat, I, 29.
Ka*m*thaka, V, 3, 68; VI, 53, 55, 67; VIII, 3, 17, 19, 32, 38, 43, 73, 75.
Kapi*m*galâda, IV, 77.
Kapila, I, 2; XII, 21.
Kapilavastu, I, 2 (?), 94; V, 84; VI, 30, 51; VIII, 5; XVII, 20, 30.
Kama*n*dalu, XV, 96.
Kamalâ, XVII, 13.
Karâlaganaka, IV, 80.
Kâma, III, 24; IV, 4; XIII, 2, 72.
Kâmâva*k*arâ*h*, the, XIV, 88.
Kârttikeya (sha*n*mukha), I, 93.
Kâla, XII, 113.
Kâlâma, XII, 2.
Kâlî, IV, 76.
Kâ*s*ikâ, XVII, 2.
Kâ*s*isu*m*darî, IV, 16.
Kâ*s*î, Kâ*s*i, XV, 89, 90, 101; XVII, 2, 6.

---

[1] This Index omits some of the obscure names in the last book.

Kaśyapa, XVII, 12.
Kaśyapas, the, XVII, 8.
Kurus, the, XI, 31.
Kuvera, I, 94; IV, 10; V, 45, 85; XVII, 15.
Kuśika, I, 49.
Kailâsa, I, 3, 21; II, 30; X, 41.
Kolata, XVII, 10.
Kaurava, IV, 79.

Gamgâ, IX, 25; XV, 98; XVII, 7.
Gamdha, XV, 97.
Gamdhapura, XV, 97.
Gaya, XII, 87.
Gayâ, XV, 91; XVII, 8.
Garuḍa, XII, 54; XVII, 22.
Gopikâ, XVII, 27, 28, 30.
Gautama, IV, 18, 72.
Gautama (Buddha), XV, 104.
Gautamî, VIII, 24, 51; XVII, 23, 28, 30.

Ghritâkî, IV, 20.

Kamdramas, IV, 75.
Kaitraratha, IV, 78.
Kyavana, I, 48.

Khamda, Khamdaka, V, 68; VI, 4, 14, 25, 43, 65; VII, 1; VIII, 9, 23, 32, 42, 73; XVII, 17, 18.

Ganaka, I, 50; IX, 20; XII, 67.
Gayamta, IX, 5, 12.
Ginakshetra, XV, 114.
Geta, XVII, 11, 15.
Getakâraṇya, XVII, 15.
Gaigîshavya, XII, 67.

Târkshya, VI, 5.
Tushita, Tushitâḥ, the, I, 19; XIV, 89; XVI, 111.
Trayastrimsad-devâḥ, XIV, 89.
Trikavyamgikâ, XVII, 4.

Damdakas, the, XI, 31.
Daśaratha, VIII, 79, 81.
Dâśarathi, VIII, 8.
Divodâsa, XVII, 7.
Dirghânakha, XVII, 11.
Deer-park, the, XV, 87, 103, 114; XVII, 5.
Devî, I, 66.
Drumasiddha, XVII, 22.
Drumâksha, IX, 60.
Drumâhgaketu, the Moon? V, 3.

Dharmakakra (ginaga), XV, 119.
Dharmapâlin, XVII, 10.
Dharmaruki, XV, 86.
Dharmâtavî, XVII, 9.
Dhânyâyana, XVII, 10.
Dhritarâshtra, XVII, 22.
Dhriti, XVII, 3.

Namdana, III, 64.
Namdabalâ, XII, 106.
Namdâguhâ, I, 19.
Namdika, XVII, 9.
Namdin, XV, 93.
Namuki, XV, 23, 46.
Naradatta, XVII, 13.
Nalakûvara, I, 94.
Nahusha, II, 11; XI, 14, 16.
Nâlaka, XVII, 3.
Nigrodha-vana (niyagrodha), XVII, 18, 27.
Nirmâṇaratayaḥ, the, XIV, 89.
Nirmitâ bodhisattvâḥ, the, XIV, 71.
Nairamganâ, XII, 88, 105.

Pamka bhikshavaḥ, pamka-vargîyâḥ, the, XII, 89, 111; XV, 89, 104, 118 (cf. Bhadravargîyâḥ).
Padma, II, 3.
Padmakhamda, III, 63.
Padmâ (?), IV, 36.
Paranirmita-vaśavartinaḥ, the, XIV, 89.
Parâśara, IV, 76; XII, 67.
Pâmdava (mountain), X, 14, 17.
Pâmdavas, the, X, 17.
Pâmdu, IV, 79.
Punarvasû, IX, 11.
Puramdara, IV, 72; XIII, 37.
Pushya, I, 25.
Pûrna, XVII, 2, 15.
Prithu, I, 29.
Paurvikâ, XVII, 27.
Pragâpati, XII, 21.

Bali, IX, 20; XI, 16; XVII, 22.
Bâlamukhyâ, IV, 17.
Bimbisâra, XV, 100 (cf. Sreṇya); XVII, 9.
Buddhâḥ (atîtâḥ), I, 38; XIV, 75; XV, 8.
Budha, IV, 75.
Bodhidruma, XII, 112, 116; XIII, 7, 27, 32, 42, 68; XIV, 90; XVII, 12.
Bodhisattva, I, 19, 24; II, 56; IX, 30; X, 18, &c.

INDEX OF PROPER NAMES. 205

Brahmakâyikâ*h*, the, XIV, 88.
Brahman, I, 1; XII, 42, 51, 65; XV, 18, 84, 118; XVI, 93, 111; XVII, 1, 24, 30.

Bhadravargîyâ*h*, the five, XII, 89, 111; XV, 89, 104, 115 (cf. Pa*m*ka bhikshava*h*).
Bhadrâsanâni, XV, 114.
Bharadvâga, IV, 74.
Bhava, I, 93.
Bhârgava, VI, 1; IX, 2, 3.
Bhîshma, IX, 25; XI, 18.
Bh*ri*gu, I, 46.

Magadhas, the, X, 10, 41; XI, 1; XVII, 11.
Maghavat, see Indra.
Mathurâ, XVII, 4.
Manu (Vaivasvata), II, 16; VIII, 78.
Ma*m*thâlagautama, IV, 17.
Ma*m*dara, VI, 13.
Mamatâ (?), IV, 74.
Marakata, XVII, 3.
Marutvat (Indra), VIII, 13; X, 39.
Maruts, the, IV, 74; V, 27.
Mahâkautuka, XVII, 27.
Mahârâgâ*h*, the, XV, 64, 74; XVII, 22.
Mahâsudar*s*a, VIII, 62.
Mahendra, see Indra.
Mahoragâ*h*, the, I, 38.
Mâdrî, IV, 79.
Mâ*m*dhât*ri*, I, 29; X, 31; XI, 13.
Mâyâ, I, 15, 22, 37; II, 18.
Mâra, XIII, 1-73; XV, 11, 37.
Mâra's sons, XIII, 3, 14.
Mâra's daughters, XIII, 3, 14; XV, 13.
Meghakâlî, XIII, 49.
Meru, V, 37, 43; XIII, 41, 57; XV, 32.
Maitra, XVII, 2, 27.
Maitrâya*n*î, XVII, 2.
Maitrîya, XV, 118; XVI, 1.
Maitreya, VII, 53.
Maithilas, the, XI, 31.
Maudgalya, XVII, 10.

Yakshâdhipâ*h*, the, I, 36.
Yamunâ, IV, 76; XII, 107.
Yayâti, II, 11; IV, 78.
Ya*s*oda, XVII, 5.
Ya*s*odr*ih*, XVII, 17.
Ya*s*odharâ, II, 26, 46; VI, 34; VIII, 31, 60, 71.
Yâmâ*h*, the, XIV, 89; XVI, 110.

Raghu, VI, 36.

Râgag*ri*ha, X, 1, 9.
Râgageha, XVII, 9, 12, 16.
Râma (Dâ*s*arathi), VI, 36; VIII, 81; IX, 9, 25, 59, 67.
Râma (Bhârgava), IX, 25.
Râhu, II, 46; IX, 28.
Râhula, II, 46; VIII, 67; IX, 28; XVII, 27, 28, 30.
Rudraka, XV, 89; XVII, 14 (cf. Udraka).
Raivata, XVII, 14.
Rohi*n*î, IV, 73.
Rohitavastuka, XV, 96.

Lumbinî, I, 23; XVII, 27.
Lopamudrâ, IV, 73.

Va*g*rabâhu, IX, 20.
Va*n*arâ, XV, 94.
Vara*n*â, XVII, 5.
Valabhid (Indra), X, 41.
Va*s*avartinâ*h*, the, XVI, 111.
Va*s*isht*h*a, I, 47, 57; IV, 77; IX, 60.
Vasus, the, VII, 7.
Vâmadeva, IX, 9.
Vârâ*n*asî, XV, 87, 101; XVII, 6.
Vâlmîki, I, 48.
Videhas, the, IX, 20.
Vidyâkara, XVII, 4.
Vindhya, XIII, 38; XVII, 3.
Vindhya-kosht*h*a, VII, 54.
Vi*s*vâ*k*î, IV, 78.
Vi*s*vâmitra, IV, 20.
Vish*n*u, XVII, 21, 24, 30.
Vu*m*da, XV, 95.
Vu*m*dadvîra, XV, 95.
V*ri*tra, VIII, 13; XI, 14.
V*ri*sh*n*is, the, XI, 31.
V*ri*hatphalâ*h*, the, XII, 58.
V*ri*haspati, I, 46; IV, 74, 75; VII, 43; IX, 12.
Ve*n*uvana, XVII, 16.
Ve*n*uvihâra, XVII, 17.
Vaibhrâga, IX, 20.
Vai*s*va*m*tara hermitage, the, XI, 73.
Vyâsa, I, 47.

*S*akti, XVII, 13.
*S*akra, see Indra.
Sa*m*khamedhîya (udyâna), XV, 102.
Sa*k*î, II, 27.
Sâkya, Sâkyas, the, I, 7, 14, 54, 63, 93; II, 25, 27; V, 1, 36; VI, 60; VII, 13; VIII, 8; IX, 11, 24; X, 11; XIII, 43; XV, 44, 85, 88; XVII, 1, 24.

Sa*m*tanu, XIII, 12.
Sâ*m*tâ, IV, 19.
Sâliputra, XVII, 11.
Sâli, XVII, 10.
Sâlyâ, XVII, 10.
Sâlvas, the, IX, 60.
Sibi, XIV, 30.
Siva, see I*s*vara.
Sukra, I, 46; IX, 10.
Suddhâdhivâsâ*h*, the, I, 39; III, 26, 56; XIII, 31.
Suddhâvâsâ*h*, the, XIV, 88.
Suddhodana, I, 9, 20; XVII, 17, 23.
Subhak*r*itsnâ*h*, the, XII, 56.
Sûra, I, 50.
Sauddhodani, II, 46; III, 40; XI, 1.
Sauri (K*r*ish*n*a), I, 50.
S*r*âvastî, XVII, 15.
S*r*e*n*ya, X, 10, 16 (cf. Bi*m*bisâra).
Svetabâlârka, XVII, 4.

Sagara, I, 49.
Sa*m*gayin, XVII, 3.
Sanatkumâra, II, 27; V, 27.
Saptarshitârâ, I, 33.
Sabhya, XVII, 4.

Sama*m*takusuma, XV, 5.
Sarvârthasiddha, II, 17; VII, 1.
Sâ*m*k*r*iti, IX, 60.
Sârathi (pura), XV, 98.
Sârasvata, I, 47.
Sugâtâ, XVII, 9.
Sudar*s*ana, XV, 92.
Sunirmitâ*h*, the, XVI, 111.
Su*m*da, XI, 32.
Su*m*darânanda, XVII, 27.
Sumitra (Sumantra?), VI, 36.
Suvar*n*anisht*h*îvin, VIII, 77.
Sûryaka, XIII, 11.
S*r*i*m*gaya (Sa*m*gaya?), VIII, 77.
Senagit, IX, 20.
Soma, IV, 73.
Sautasomî, XVII, 27.
Saunu, Saunava (?), XVII, 28, 30.
Svaya*m*bhû, II, 51; X, 2, 19; XVII, 30.
Svastika, XVII, 6.

Hari (see Vish*n*u), XV, 103.
Himavat, I, 20; II, 3; IV, 27; V, 45; VIII, 36; IX, 68; XVII, 13.

NOTES AND CORRECTIONS.

Page 11, note 2 (I, 63). Professor Jacobi writes, 'Indra's banner is intimately connected with the *G*aina legend of king Domuha (see my Ausgew. Erzähl. in Mâhârâsh*t*rî, p. 40); the old *G*aina legends originated in the East; cf. also Râmây. II, 74, 36; IV, 16, 37; 17, 2 (Bombay ed.).'

P. 21, l. 30 (II, 31 *b*). I have read in the translation madai*h* for the printed ma*m*dai*h*.

P. 33, l. 30 (III, 50 *c*). If we read api nâma sakto, the translation should run, 'would that he might not be able to forsake us, even though he remained attached to us only through the restlessness of the senses.'

P. 49, note 2, l. 4, read kumude*s*a.

P. 60, l. 31 (V, 80 *d*). This might be rendered 'planting his footsteps without alarm,' but I have taken *k*akita as meaning 'hurrying' from the *k*akitagate*h* of the next *s*loka.

P. 83 (VIII, 31 *d*), add to note 2, 'there is a similar confusion of vigâdha and vigâ*dh*a in the MSS. in VIII, 76.'

INDEX OF NAMES AND SUBJECTS
IN THE AMITÂYUR-DHYÂNA-SÛTRA.

Abhi*tb*ânam, page 192 note; 198 note.
Agâta*s*atru, 161; 162; 164.
Amitâbha (or Amitâyus), 166; 195.
Amitâyus (or Amitâbha), 166; 167; 169; 176; 180; 189; 195; 198; 200; 201.
Anâgâmin, 167.
Ânanda, 164; 165; 168; 179, et passim.
Ânantarya sins, p. 198 note.
Anutpatikadharmakshânti, 169 note.
Anuttarasa*m*yaksa*m*bodhi, 191.
Arhat, 178; 195.
Arhatghâta, 197 note.
Asankhya kalpas, 185.
Avaivartya, 191.
Avalokite*s*vara, 176, et passim.

Bhagavat, see World-Honoured One.
Bhikshus, 161; 175; 177; 189.
Bimbisâra, 161; 167.
Bodhi, 168; 191; 196; 197; 199; the circle of, 200 note.
Bodhi-ma*nd*ala, 200.
Bodhisattvas, 161, et passim.
Brahma-ma*n*i, 176.
Brahman (god), 165; 172.
Brute creation, 165; 182 note; 184.
Buddha, spiritual body of, 178; the height of Buddha *S*âkyamuni, 187; the charity of, 188.

Chiliocosm, 173; 180.

Depravities (five), 165 note.
Devadatta, 161; 165.
Dhâra*n*î, 190.

Dharmadhâtu-kâya, 178.
Dharmâkara, 177; 194.

Enlightenment, the round terrace of, 200.
Existence, the five paths of, 182; non-, 171; 174; 193.

Five deadly sins, 192; 197 note.

*G*ambudvîpa, 165.
*G*âmbûnada (gold), 173; 176; 178; 180; 182.
Gangâ, 180.
Garlands, 162; 163, et passim.
*G*îva, famous physician, 163; 164.
Gri*dh*rakû*t*a, 161; 162; 164; 201.

Hardy (Spence), 187 note.
Hells, 165; 182 note; 184.
Hungry spirits (Pretas), 165; 182 note.

Impermanence, 171; 174; 193.
Indra, 165; 173.

Kâlaya*s*as, a *S*rama*n*a from India, 161.
*K*and*â*la, 164.
*K*andraprabha, minister of king Bimbisâra, 163.
Karma, 183; 200.
Karmâvara*n*a-vi*s*uddhi, 200 note.
K'-*k*ö (Chisha-daishi of Ten-dai), 161 note.
Kim*s*uka, 176.
*K*intâma*n*i, 174 note.
Kshânti (Anutpatikadharma-), 169.

Kshatriyas (the kingly race), 163.
Kumârabhûta, 161 note.

Lapis lazuli, 169, et passim.
Law, prince of the, 161; remembrance of the, 174; eternal Law, 169 note.

Mahâmaudgalyâyana (mokuren), 162; 163; 164; 165; 201.
Mahâsthâma, 176; named Unlimited Light, 184, et passim.
Mahâvyutpatti, 197 note.
Mahâyâna, 168; 188; 190; 191; 195; 197.
Mahesvara Deva, 166.
Mañgusri, 161.
Marks (minor), 174.
Mâtrighâta, 197 note.
Meditation, 167, et passim.

Nâga, 201.
Nirvâna, 167; 169; 194.
Noble Truths (the four), 193.
Non-existence, 171; 174; 193.
Non-self, 171; 174; 193.

Padma (lotus), 184.
Pâramitâ, 174.
Pitrighâta, 197 note.
Prayer, of Dharmâkara, 177; mystic form of, 190; the forty-eight, 194.
Precepts, the eight prohibitive, 162; 192; the ten prohibitive, 167 note; the five prohibitive, 192.
Pretas, 165; 184.
Pundarika, 200.
Pûrna (Furuna), 162.

Râgagriha, 161.
Remembrance (sixfold), 188; of the Buddha, 174, et passim.
Resignation (spirit of), 169; 181; 189; 191; 199.

Saddharmapundarika, 161; 200 note.
Sakra (Indra), 165; 173; 176.
Sakrâbhilagnamaniratna, 173 note.
Sâkyamuni, 165; 182; the height of, 187 note; 201.
Samâdhi, 171; 181; 191; 199.
Sanghabheda, 197 note.
Sanghika lâbha, 196.
Satadharmavidyâdvâra, 192; 196 (where the Sanskrit is omitted).
Scriptures, the twelve divisions of, 186; 195.
Shân-tâo (Jen-do Daishi), 162; 163 note.
Signs of perfection, 174; 178.
Siva, 166.
Spells, 163.
Sramanas, 163.
Sramanera (a novice), 193.
Srâvakas, 189.
Srota-âpanna, 194.
Sufferings, the five worldly, 169; 171; 174; 193.
Sukhâvatî, 166; 167; 168; 171; 175; 185; 200.
Sumeru, 166; 177; 180.

Tathâgata (Nyo-rai), 164; 178; 187.
Tathâgatasyântike dushtakittarudhirotpâdana, 197 note.
Three Jewels (Ratna-traya), 167; 188 note; 196.

Ushnîshasiraskatâ, 182.

Vaidehî, consort of Bimbisâra, 161; 164, et passim.
Vaipulya Sûtra, 188; 190; 195.
Veda, 163.

World-Honoured One, 162; 164, et passim, being a translation of Bhagavat, the Blessed One.

Yaksha, 201.
Yama, 177; 180.

TRANSLITERATION OF ORIENTAL ALPHABETS ADOPTED FOR THE TRANSLATIONS OF THE SACRED BOOKS OF THE EAST.

CONSONANTS	MISSIONARY ALPHABET.			Sanskrit.	Zend.	Pehlevi.	Persian.	Arabic.	Hebrew.	Chinese.
	I Class.	II Class.	III Class.							
Gutturales.										
1 Tenuis	k			क		ﻖ	ﻙ	ﻙ	כ	k
2 „ aspirata	kh			ख					ח	kh
3 Media	g			ग		ﻝ	ﻍ		ד	
4 „ aspirata	gh			घ		ﻎ	ﻎ		ג	
5 Gutturo-labialis	q								ק	
6 Nasalis	ṅ (ng)			ङ	ŋ (ng) w (n)					
7 Spiritus asper	h			ह	ŋ (ŋhw)	ŋ				h, hs
8 „ lenis	ʼ								ה	
9 „ asper faucalis	ḥ								ח	
10 „ lenis faucalis	ʽh								ע	
11 „ asper fricatus		ʼh								
12 „ lenis fricatus		ʽh								
Gutturales modificatae (palatales, &c.)										
13 Tenuis		k		च		ﺝ	ﻉ			k
14 „ aspirata		kh		छ		ﻉ	ﻉ	ﻉ		kh
15 Media		g		ज	ᴣ		ﻍ	ﻍ		
16 „ aspirata		gh		झ						
17 „ Nasalis		ñ		ञ						

206 TRANSLITERATION OF ORIENTAL ALPHABETS

CONSONANTS (continued)	MISSIONARY ALPHABET.			Sanskrit.	Zend.	Pehlevi.	Persian.	Arabic.	Hebrew.	Chinese.
	I Class.	II Class.	III Class.							
18 Semivocalis	y			य	३	ر	ی	ی	ו	y
19 Spiritus asper		(y)								
20 " lenis		(y)								
21 " asper assibilatus		s		श	४ ह	۴ ف	۫ڑ	۫ڑ		s
22 " lenis assibilatus		z								
Dentales.										
23 Tenuis	t			त त	६ ष	٢	٥	٥	תת	t
24 " aspirata	th		TH							th
25 " assibilata										
26 Media	d			द द	८ ر	٥	ر	ر	ךד	d
27 " aspirata	dh		DH							
28 " assibilata										
29 Nasalis	n			न ज	۷	ن	ن	ن	נן	n
30 Semivocalis	l			ल ळ	٢٫۱	۷٫ئ،۱				l
31 " mollis 1		ı	L							
32 " mollis 2										
33 Spiritus asper 1	s		S	स	३	४	ڈ	ڈ	ם ס	s
34 " asper 2										
35 " lenis	z				ى	ى	j(z)	ز	ז	z, zh

FOR THE SACRED BOOKS OF THE EAST. 207

						⌐	sh		p	ph			m	w		⌐		
ɔ				⌐					⊓ ⊓ ⊓ ⊓		⊓				⌐		
ᛋ	ᛋ	ᚴ	⌐						}		⌒		]	⌒	
ᛋ	ᛋ		⌐				}	}		⌒		]	⌒	
	ᖳ	ᓚᑫ	ᑐ			ᑐ	ᑐ	ᓚ		ᓚ		ᑐ	ᑐᐧᑕ	
	ᖳ	ᔆ	ᑐ			ᑐ	ᓚ		ᓚ		«	ᔆ	
ᘔ	ᘔ	ᘔ	ᘔ	ᐛ		ᐛ		ᐛ ᐛ ᐛ ᐛ		ᐛ			ᐛ ᐛ	
						ᴙ												
t	th	d	dh	n		ɾ			p						m	h
				ɾ		sh	zh	p ph b bh		m w hw f v				

Dentales modificatae (linguales, &c.)
38 Tenuis
39 „ aspirata
40 Media
41 „ aspirata
42 Nasalis
43 Semivocalis
44 „ fricata
45 „ diacritica
46 Spiritus asper
47 „ lenis

Labiales.
48 Tenuis
49 „ aspirata
50 Media
51 „ aspirata
52 Tenuissima
53 Nasalis
54 Semivocalis
55 „ aspirata
56 Spiritus asper
57 „ lenis
58 Anusvâra
59 Visarga

208 TRANSLITERATION OF ORIENTAL ALPHABETS.

VOWELS.	MISSIONARY ALPHABET.			Sanskrit.	Zend.	Pehlevi.	Persian.	Arabic.	Hebrew.	Chinese.
	I Class.	II Class.	III Class.							
1 Neutralis	o									֑	
2 Laryngo-palatalis	ă					ܐ fin. ܐ init.				ְ	ă
3 " labialis	ŏ				ڒ	ܒ	ا	ا		ֳ	ā
4 Gutturalis brevis	a	(a)		अ	ܙ					ָ	̄
5 " longa	â			आ	ܡ					ֶ	̂
6 Palatalis brevis	i	(i)		इ	ܢ						
7 " longa	î			ई	ܓ						
8 Dentalis brevis	ĭ										
9 " longa	ī										
10 Lingualis brevis	ri			ऋ							
11 " longa	rî			ॠ							
12 Labialis brevis	u	(u)		उ		ܒ					u
13 " longa	û			ऊ	ᐊ			ـ	ـ	|ו̇| ŏ
14 Gutturo-palatalis brevis	e	(e)			ε(e) ξ(e) λ	ܓ				ְ	e
15 " longa	ê (ai)	(ai)									ĕ
16 Diphthongus gutturo-palatalis	âi										ai, ei
17 " "	ei (êi)										
18 " "	oi (ôu)										
19 Gutturo-labialis brevis	o	(o)			ᐱ	ܐ				וֹ	o
20 " longa	ô (au)			ओ	ᐲ (au)		ـ	ـ		וּ	
21 Diphthongus gutturo-labialis	âu	(au)		औ							áu
22 " "	eu (êu)										
23 " "	ou (ôu)										
24 Gutturalis fracta	ä										
25 Palatalis fracta	ï										
26 Labialis fracta	ü										ü
27 Gutturo-labialis fracta	ö										

Sacred Books of the East

TRANSLATED BY

VARIOUS ORIENTAL SCHOLARS

AND EDITED BY

F. MAX MÜLLER

⁎⁎⁎ This Series is published with the sanction and co-operation of the Secretary of State for India in Council.

REPORT presented to the ACADÉMIE DES INSCRIPTIONS, May 11, 1883, by M. ERNEST RENAN.

'M. Renan présente trois nouveaux volumes de la grande collection des "Livres sacrés de l'Orient" (Sacred Books of the East), que dirige à Oxford, avec une si vaste érudition et une critique si sûre, le savant associé de l'Académie des Inscriptions, M. Max Müller. . . . La première série de ce beau recueil, composée de 24 volumes, est presque achevée. M. Max Müller se propose d'en publier une seconde, dont l'intérêt historique et religieux ne sera pas moindre. M. Max Müller a su se procurer la collaboration des savans les plus éminens d'Europe et d'Asie. L'Université d'Oxford, que cette grande publication honore au plus haut degré, doit tenir à continuer dans les plus larges proportions une œuvre aussi philosophiquement conçue que savamment exécutée.'

EXTRACT from the QUARTERLY REVIEW.

'We rejoice to notice that a second series of these translations has been announced and has actually begun to appear. The stones, at least, out of which a stately edifice may hereafter arise, are here being brought together. Prof. Max Müller has deserved well of scientific history. Not a few minds owe to his enticing words their first attraction to this branch of study. But no work of his, not even the great edition of the Rig-Veda, can compare in importance or in usefulness with this English translation of the Sacred Books of the East, which has been devised by his foresight, successfully brought so far by his persuasive and organising power, and will, we trust, by the assistance of the distinguished scholars he has gathered round him, be carried in due time to a happy completion.'

Professor E. HARDY, Inaugural Lecture in the University of Freiburg, 1887.

'Die allgemeine vergleichende Religionswissenschaft datirt von jenem grossartigen, in seiner Art einzig dastehenden Unternehmen, zu welchem auf Anregung Max Müllers im Jahre 1874 auf dem internationalen Orientalistencongress in London der Grundstein gelegt worden war, die Übersetzung der heiligen Bücher des Ostens' (*the Sacred Books of the East*).

The Hon. ALBERT S. G. CANNING 'Words on Existing Religions.'

'The recent publication of the "Sacred Works of the East" in English is surely a great event in the annals of theological literature.'

Oxford
AT THE CLARENDON PRESS

LONDON: HENRY FROWDE

OXFORD UNIVERSITY PRESS WAREHOUSE, AMEN CORNER, E.C.

FIRST SERIES.

VOL. I. The Upanishads.
  Translated by F. MAX MÜLLER. Part I. The *K*hândogya-upanishad, The Talavakâra-upanishad, The Aitareya-âra*n*yaka, The Kaushîtaki-brâhma*n*a-upanishad, and The Vâgasaneyi-samhitâ-upanishad. 8vo, cloth, 10s. 6d.

The Upanishads contain the philosophy of the Veda. They have become the foundation of the later Vedânta doctrines, and indirectly of Buddhism. Schopenhauer, speaking of the Upanishads, says: 'In the whole world there is no study so beneficial and so elevating as that of the Upanishads. It has been the solace of my life, it will be the solace of my death.'

[See also Vol. XV.]

VOL. II. The Sacred Laws of the Âryas,
  As taught in the Schools of Âpastamba, Gautama, Vâsish*th*a, and Baudhâyana. Translated by GEORG BÜHLER. Part I. Âpastamba and Gautama. 8vo, cloth, 10s. 6d.

The Sacred Laws of the Âryas contain the original treatises on which the Laws of Manu and other lawgivers were founded.

[See also Vol. XIV.]

VOL. III. The Sacred Books of China.
  The Texts of Confucianism. Translated by JAMES LEGGE. Part I. The Shû King, The Religious Portions of the Shih King, and The Hsiâo King. 8vo, cloth, 12s. 6d.

Confucius was a collector of ancient traditions, not the founder of a new religion. As he lived in the sixth and fifth centuries B.C. his works are of unique interest for the study of Ethology.

[See also Vols. XVI, XXVII, XXVIII, XXXIX, and XL.]

VOL. IV. The Zend-Avesta.
  Translated by JAMES DARMESTETER. Part I. The Vendîdâd. 8vo, cloth, 10s. 6d.

The Zend-Avesta contains the relics of what was the religion of Cyrus, Darius, and Xerxes, and, but for the battle of Marathon, might have become the religion of Europe. It forms to the present day the sacred book of the Parsis, the so-called fire-worshippers. Two more volumes will complete the translation of all that is left us of Zoroaster's religion.

[See also Vols. XXIII and XXXI.]

VOL. V. Pahlavi Texts.
Translated by E. W. WEST. Part I. The Bundahis, Bahman Yast, and Shâyast lâ-shâyast. 8vo, cloth, 12s. 6d.

The Pahlavi Texts comprise the theological literature of the revival of Zoroaster's religion, beginning with the Sassanian dynasty. They are important for a study of Gnosticism.

VOLS. VI AND IX. The Qur'ân.
Parts I and II. Translated by E. H. PALMER. 8vo, cloth, 21s.

This translation, carried out according to his own peculiar views of the origin of the Qur'ân, was the last great work of E. H. Palmer, before he was murdered in Egypt.

VOL. VII. The Institutes of Vishnu.
Translated by JULIUS JOLLY. 8vo, cloth, 10s. 6d.

A collection of legal aphorisms, closely connected with one of the oldest Vedic schools, the Kathas, but considerably added to in later time. Of importance for a critical study of the Laws of Manu.

VOL. VIII. The Bhagavadgîtâ, with The Sanatsugâtîya, and The Anugîtâ.
Translated by KÂSHINÂTH TRIMBAK TELANG. 8vo, cloth, 10s. 6d.

The earliest philosophical and religious poem of India. It has been paraphrased in Arnold's 'Song Celestial.'

VOL. X. The Dhammapada,
Translated from Pâli by F. MAX MÜLLER; and
The Sutta-Nipâta,
Translated from Pâli by V. FAUSBÖLL; being Canonical Books of the Buddhists. 8vo, cloth, 10s. 6d.

The Dhammapada contains the quintessence of Buddhist morality. The Sutta-Nipâta gives the authentic teaching of Buddha on some of the fundamental principles of religion.

Vol. XI. Buddhist Suttas.
Translated from Pâli by T. W. Rhys Davids. 1. The Mahâparinibbâna Suttanta; 2. The Dhamma-*k*akka-ppavattana Sutta. 3. The Tevi*gg*a Suttanta; 4. The Âkankheyya Sutta; 5. The *K*etokhila Sutta; 6. The Mahâ-sudassana Suttanta; 7. The Sabbâsava Sutta. 8vo, cloth, 10s. 6d.

A collection of the most important religious, moral, and philosophical discourses taken from the sacred canon of the Buddhists.

Vol. XII. The *S*atapatha-Brâhma*n*a, according to the Text of the Mâdhyandina School.
Translated by Julius Eggeling. Part I. Books I and II. 8vo, cloth, 12s. 6d.

A minute account of the sacrificial ceremonies of the Vedic age. It contains the earliest account of the Deluge in India.
[See also Vols. XXVI, XLI.]

Vol. XIII. Vinaya Texts.
Translated from the Pâli by T. W. Rhys Davids and Hermann Oldenberg. Part I. The Pâtimokkha. The Mahâvagga, I-IV. 8vo, cloth, 10s. 6d.

The Vinaya Texts give for the first time a translation of the moral code of the Buddhist religion as settled in the third century B.C.
[See also Vols. XVII and XX.]

Vol. XIV. The Sacred Laws of the Âryas,
As taught in the Schools of Âpastamba, Gautama, Vâsish*th*a, and Baudhâyana. Translated by Georg Bühler. Part II. Vasish*th*a and Baudhâyana. 8vo, cloth, 10s. 6d.

Vol. XV. The Upanishads.
Translated by F. Max Müller. Part II. The Ka*th*a-upanishad, The Mu*nd*aka-upanishad, The Taittirîyaka-upanishad, The B*ri*hadâra*n*yaka-upanishad, The *S*vetâsvatara-upanishad, The Pra*sn*a-upanishad, and The Maitrâya*n*a-brâhma*n*a-upanishad. 8vo, cloth, 10s. 6d.

Vol. XVI. The Sacred Books of China.
The Texts of Confucianism. Translated by James Legge. Part II. The Yî King. 8vo, cloth, 10s. 6d.
[See also Vols. XXVII, XXVIII.]

Vol. XVII. Vinaya Texts.
Translated from the Pâli by T. W. Rhys Davids and Hermann Oldenberg. Part II. The Mahâvagga V-X. The *K*ullavagga, I-III. 8vo, cloth, 10s. 6d.

VOL. XVIII. Pahlavi Texts.
  Translated by E. W. West. Part II. The Dâdistân-î Dînik and The Epistles of Mânûskîhar. 8vo, cloth, 12s. 6d.

VOL. XIX. The Fo-sho-hing-tsan-king.
  A Life of Buddha by Asvaghosha Bodhisattva, translated from Sanskrit into Chinese by Dharmaraksha, A.D. 420, and from Chinese into English by SAMUEL BEAL. 8vo, cloth, 10s. 6d.

  This life of Buddha was translated from Sanskrit into Chinese, A.D. 420. It contains many legends, some of which show a certain similarity to the Evangelium infantiae, &c.

VOL. XX. Vinaya Texts.
  Translated from the Pâli by T. W. RHYS DAVIDS and HERMANN OLDENBERG. Part III. The Kullavagga, IV–XII. 8vo, cloth, 10s. 6d.

VOL. XXI. The Saddharma-pundarîka; or, The Lotus of the True Law.
  Translated by H. KERN. 8vo, cloth, 12s. 6d.

  'The Lotus of the true Law,' a canonical book of the Northern Buddhists, translated from Sanskrit. There is a Chinese translation of this book which was finished as early as the year 286 A.D.

VOL. XXII. Gaina-Sûtras.
  Translated from Prâkrit by HERMANN JACOBI. Part I. The Âkârânga-Sûtra and The Kalpa-Sûtra. 8vo, cloth, 10s. 6d.

  The religion of the Gainas was founded by a contemporary of Buddha. It still counts numerous adherents in India, while there are no Buddhists left in India proper.

  Part II, *in preparation.*

VOL. XXIII. The Zend-Avesta.
  Translated by JAMES DARMESTETER. Part II. The Sîrôzahs, Yasts, and Nyâyis. 8vo, cloth, 10s. 6d.

VOL. XXIV. Pahlavi Texts.
  Translated by E. W. WEST. Part III. Dînâ-î Maînôg-Khirad, Sikand-gûmânîk Vigâr, and Sad Dar. 8vo, cloth, 10s. 6d.

SECOND SERIES.

VOL. XXV. Manu.
Translated by GEORG BÜHLER. 8vo, cloth, 21s.
This translation is founded on that of Sir William Jones, which has been carefully revised and corrected with the help of seven native Commentaries. An Appendix contains all the quotations from Manu which are found in the Hindu Law-books, translated for the use of the Law Courts in India. Another Appendix gives a synopsis of parallel passages from the six Dharma-sûtras, the other Sm*ri*tis, the Upanishads, the Mahâbhârata, &c.

VOL. XXVI. The Satapatha-Brâhma*n*a.
Translated by JULIUS EGGELING. Part II. Books III and IV. 8vo, cloth, 12s. 6d.

VOLS. XXVII AND XXVIII. The Sacred Books of China.
The Texts of Confucianism. Translated by JAMES LEGGE. Parts III and IV. The Lî *K*î, or Collection of Treatises on the Rules of Propriety, or Ceremonial Usages. 8vo, cloth, 12s. 6d. each.

VOL. XXIX. The G*ri*hya-Sûtras, Rules of Vedic Domestic Ceremonies.
Part I. Sânkhâyana, Âsvalâyana, Pâraskara, Khâdira. Translated by HERMANN OLDENBERG. 8vo, cloth, 12s. 6d.
These rules of Domestic Ceremonies describe the home life of the ancient Âryas with a completeness and accuracy unmatched in any other literature. Some of these rules have been incorporated in the ancient Law-books.

VOL. XXX. The G*ri*hya-Sûtras, Rules of Vedic Domestic Ceremonies.
Part II. Gobhila, Hira*n*yakesin, Âpastamba. Translated by HERMANN OLDENBERG. Âpastamba, Yag*ñ*a-paribhâshâ-sûtras. Translated by F. MAX MÜLLER. 8vo, cloth, 12s. 6d.

VOL. XXXI. The Zend-Avesta.
Part III. The Yasna, Visparad, Âfrînagân, Gâhs, and Miscellaneous Fragments. Translated by L. H. MILLS. 8vo, cloth, 12s. 6d.

VOL. XXXII. Vedic Hymns.
Translated by F. MAX MÜLLER. Part I. 8vo, cloth, 18s. 6d.

Vol. XXXIII. The Minor Law-books.
Translated by JULIUS JOLLY. Part I. Nârada, Br*i*haspati. 8vo, cloth, 10s. 6d.

Vol. XXXIV. The Vedânta-Sûtras, with the Commentary by *S*ankara*k*ârya. Part I.
Translated by G. THIBAUT. 8vo, cloth, 12s. 6d.

Vol. XXXV. The Questions of King Milinda. Part I.
Translated from the Pâli by T. W. RHYS DAVIDS. 8vo, cloth, 10s. 6d.

Vol. XXXVI. The Questions of King Milinda. Part II.
[*In the Press.*]

Vol. XXXVII. The Contents of the Nasks, as stated in the Eighth and Ninth Books of the Dinka*r*d.
Part I. Translated by E. W. WEST. 8vo, cloth, 15s.

Vol. XXXVIII. The Vedânta-Sûtras. Part II. [*In the Press.*]

Vols. XXXIX and XL. The Sacred Books of China.
The Texts of Tâoism. Translated by JAMES LEGGE. 8vo, cloth, 21s.

Vol. XLI. The *S*atapatha-Brâhma*n*a. Part III. Translated by JULIUS EGGELING. [*In the Press.*]

Vol. XLII. The Buddha-*k*arita. Translated by E. B. COWELL. The Sukhâvatî-vyûha. Translated by F. MAX MÜLLER. [*In the Press.*]

Vols. XLIII and XLIV. The *S*atapatha-Brâhma*n*a.
Parts IV and V. [*In preparation.*]

Vol. XLV. The *G*aina-Sûtras. Part II. [*In preparation.*]

Vol. XLVI. The Vedânta-Sûtras. Part III. [*In preparation.*]

Vol. XLVII. The Contents of the Nasks. Part II. [*In preparation.*]

Vol. XLVIII. Vedic Hymns. Part II. [*In preparation.*]

Anecdota Oxoniensia.

ARYAN SERIES.

Buddhist Texts from Japan. I. Vagra*kkh*edikâ; *The Diamond-Cutter.*
> Edited by F. Max Müller, M.A. Small 4to, 3s. 6d.
> One of the most famous metaphysical treatises of the Mahâyâna Buddhists.

Buddhist Texts from Japan. II. Sukhâvatî-Vyûha: *Description of Sukhâvatî, the Land of Bliss.*
> Edited by F. Max Müller, M.A., and Bunyiu Nanjio. With two Appendices: (1) Text and Translation of Sanghavarman's Chinese Version of the Poetical Portions of the Sukhâvatî-Vyûha; (2) Sanskrit Text of the Smaller Sukhâvatî-Vyûha. Small 4to, 7s. 6d.
> The *editio princeps* of the Sacred Book of one of the largest and most influential sects of Buddhism, numbering more than ten millions of followers in Japan alone.

Buddhist Texts from Japan. III. *The Ancient Palm-Leaves containing the* Pragñâ-Pâramitâ-H*ri*daya-Sûtra *and the* Ush*n*isha-Vi*g*aya-Dhâra*n*î.
> Edited by F. Max Müller, M.A., and Bunyiu Nanjio, M.A. With an Appendix by G. Bühler, C.I.E. With many Plates. Small 4to, 10s.
> Contains facsimiles of the oldest Sanskrit MS. at present known.

Dharma-Sa*m*graha, *an Ancient Collection of Buddhist Technical Terms.*
> Prepared for publication by Kenjiu Kasawara, a Buddhist Priest from Japan, and, after his death, edited by F. Max Müller and H. Wenzel. Small 4to, 7s. 6d.

Kâtâyana's Sarvânukrama*n*î of the *Ri*gveda.
> With Extracts from Sha*d*guru*s*ishya's Commentary entitled Vedârthadîpikâ. Edited by A. A. Macdonell, M.A., Ph.D. 16s.

Oxford
AT THE CLARENDON PRESS

LONDON: HENRY FROWDE
OXFORD UNIVERSITY PRESS WAREHOUSE, AMEN CORNER, E.C.

www.ingramcontent.com/pod-product-compliance
Lightning Source LLC
Chambersburg PA
CBHW021811230426
43669CB00008B/708